BOEING 747

P.R. SMITH

Printed in Singapore by Kyodo-Shing Loong Printing Inds PTE Ltd.

Airlife Publishing Ltd.

101 Longden Road, Shrewsbury, England.

Introduction

Not many people would have believed that they would see the roll-out of the world's largest commercial airliner on September 30 1968, only thirty-five years after Boeing's Model 247 had made its first flight. So much had happened between those years, from the post war Model 307 'Stratoliner', to the 'Jumbo' of its era, the Model 377 'Stratocruiser'. With the advent of the pure jet, design work lead to the four-engined Boeing 707, long-range airliner. Then there were the hugely successful Boeing 737 and 727, with two and three engines respectively.

From the late 1950s the idea of a large civilian passenger transport, capable of flying very long distances, had been talked about by the world's major airlines. It was not however, until January 1966 that the first detailed proposals for the 747 were made public. Initial designs called for three separate aircraft, with overall lengths of 49.38 m (162 ft) (designated as the 747-4); 52.73 m (173 ft) (747-3), and 57 m (187 ft) (747-5). All shared a common 'double deck' fuselage cross section, with seating capacity for 311, 363 and 433 passengers respectively. During the months that followed, Boeing began to rethink the basic shape, following customer reaction to its original proposal. By the time details were finally announced in April 1966, a single main deck had been incorporated. The aircraft had grown considerably to accommodate 490 passengers. The single, most important, change to the entire programme was when Pan American placed an order for twenty-five units, thus confirming beyond any doubt that this formula was indeed the right one to follow.

The first Boeing 747 took to the skies on February 9 1969, under the command of Jack Waddell, test pilot. A planned two-and-a-half hour inaugural flight was cut short by some minor leading edge problems. However, everybody on board was delighted by the general handling qualities of the aircraft.

As soon as the 747 had settled down into regular commercial service, Boeing began the serious process of developing the type's full potential. Certification weight was increased from the original 322,056 kg (710,000 lb) to 333,396 kg (735,000 lb). This increase was subsequently approved, and aircraft from airframe 62 took up this extra allowance. Due to the increase in weight, it was possible to take on fuel for an additional 644 km (400 miles) of range. The upgraded 747B made its debut flight on October 11 1970. At the same time Boeing announced details of a new, extended life, 747 which was aimed at the high capacity domestic Japanese market. British European Airways had also shown an interest in it, for use on domestic routes. However, the order finally went to Lockheed for its 1011 Tristar. By the end of 1972 five models were available, the SR — Short Range, the 333,396 kg (735,000 lb) original 747-100, the 351,540 kg (775,000 lb) standard 747-200; the 747-200F, a dedicated 'freighter' variant; and a 747-200C convertible passenger/cargo aircraft.

In August 1973, Boeing announced details of its 747SP (Special Performance), and by September of that year Pan American had placed orders and options for twenty-five aircraft (it was to follow in later years that the company would cancel most of the order in favour of other types). Designed as a direct attack on the long range markets dominated by Douglas and its DC-10, Series 30 and 40 types, the aircraft was a significant departure from the familiar 747 formula. However, over ninety per cent commonality was retained with earlier examples. Basically, the SP was a shortened 747-100, with fuselage and passenger capacity reduced accordingly. A first flight was achieved in July 1975, with delivery to the launch customer, the following year.

Military usage had always been a part of Boeing's plan for the 747, because it saw the aircraft as a natural successor to the KC-97 and KC-135. However, despite the greatest of efforts, nothing was forthcoming, with the exception of the E4A/B Advanced Airborne National Command Post programme. Having been based on greatly modified 747-200B airframes, these aircraft are designed to be able to fly for anything up to seventy-two hours, nonstop, in the most hostile of environments.

Probably the most unusual use of a 747 is its task as the carrier for the US Space Shuttle. A used Series 100 was purchased by NASA from American Airlines, and was sent to Boeing for structural modifications. The aircraft acts basically as a 'piggy back' ride for the Shuttle, and delivers it back to the launch site. Such is the case when the Orbiter lands at Edward's Air Force Base in California, and needs transport back to Cape Canaveral, in Florida.

In 1976 Boeing initiated design work on a stretched upper deck variant, with increased range, take-off weight, etc. Known originally as the EUD (Extended Upper Deck), this was later dropped in favour of the Series 300 designation. Passenger capacity was increased to 570, and the engines were upgraded. The first flight of this type was made in October 1982, with first deliveries to Swissair and UTA taking place the following March. In May 1985, Boeing announced the latest development of its 747 family, the Series 400. An advanced long range version of the Series 300, the aircraft has a 1.83 m (6 ft) extension to each wing tip, with a 1.83 m (6 ft) winglet. Also included are upgraded engines, two-man digital flight deck, greater flexibility of interior configurations, increased range and greater fuel economy. The prototype flew for the first time on April 29 1988. A little behind schedule, the first Series 400 was delivered to Northwest in the first quarter of 1989.

TABLE OF COMPARISONS		
	747-100	747-200
First flight date:	February 9 1969	October 11 1970
Max. accommodation:	516	516
Wing span:	59.64 m (195 ft 7 in)	59.64 m (195 ft 7 in)
Length:	70.66 m (231 ft 8 in)	70.66 m (231 ft 8 in)
Height:	19.33 m (63 ft 4 in)	19.33 m (63 ft 4 in)
Max. t/o weight:	340,195 kg (750,000 lb)	377,840 kg (833,000 lb)
Max. cruis. speed:	977 km/h (607 mph)	969 km/h (602 mph)
Maximum range:	8,895 km (5,527 miles)	13,158 km (8,176 miles)
Service ceiling:	13,715 km (45,000 ft)	13,715 m (45,000 ft)
	747-300	747-400
First flight date:	October 5 1982	April 29 1988
Max. accommodation:	538	660
Wing span:	59.64 m (195 ft 7 in)	64.30 m (211 ft 0 in)
Length:	70.66 m (231 ft 8 in)	70.70 m (231 ft 10 n)
Height:	19.33 m (63 ft 4 in)	19.33 m (63 ft 4 in)
Max. t/o weight:	377,840 kg (833,000 lb)	385,555 kg (850,000 lb)
Max. cruis. speed:	982 km/h (610 mph)	982 km/h (610 mph)
Maximum range:	10,463 km (6,502 miles)	15,410 km (8,320 miles)
Service ceiling:	13,715 km (45,000 ft)	13,715 m (45,000 ft)
	747SP	
First flight date:	July 4 1975	
Max. accommodation:	440	
Wing span:	59.64 m (195 ft 7 in)	
Length:	56.30 m (184 ft 7 in)	
Height:	20.00 m (65 ft 6 in)	
Max. t/o weight:	299,376 kg (660,000 lb)	
Max. cruis. speed:	935km/h (581 mph)	
Maximum range:	16,450 km (10,222 miles)	
Service ceiling:	13,715 km (45,000 ft)	

AER LINGUS — IRISH AIRLINES (EI/EIN)

Republic of Ireland

Aer Lingus, the national flag carrier of the Republic of Ireland, was founded on May 22 1936 by the Irish Government. With technical assistance from Blackpool and West Coast Air Services, the company initially utilized a sole de Havilland Dragon Rapide to Bristol. Eventually the carrier merged with the international Aerlinte Eireann, which itself was formed in 1947. Major shareholders are the Ministry of Finance (for the Irish Government), with a small number of qualifying shares in the hands of the company's management. Aer Lingus provides managerial and technical assistance to a large number of airlines worldwide. The carrier also has interests in hotels, catering, tourism, computer services, and robotic systems. Subsidiary companies include Irish Helicopters, Aviation Traders Engineering, Airmotive Ireland, and Guinness Peat Aviation/Air Tara. Aer Lingus operates scheduled passenger and cargo services from Dublin, Shannon and Cork to London (LHR, LGW and STN), Manchester, Birmingham, Bristol, Liverpool, East Midlands, Leeds/Bradford, Jersey, Guernsey, Edinburgh and Glasgow in the UK; Paris (CDG), Amsterdam, Frankfurt, Dusseldorf, Munich, Brussels, Zurich, Rome, Milan, Copenhagen and Madrid in Europe; and New York (JFK) and Boston in North America. A fleet of BAe 1-11, Boeing 737-200 and -300, Shorts 360, Fokker 50 and Boeing 747-100 aircraft is utilized. The Shorts 360s and Fokker 50 are however, flown by Aer Lingus Commuter. This subsidiary was formed in 1984, to cater for business and holiday traffic on the smaller domestic routes from its base at Dublin. An order is outstanding for a quantity of the new Boeing 737-400 and 737-500. The company livery, designed by King and Wetherell, reflects a bold national identity through the usage of predominantly green colouring and Irish Shamrock logos. The fuselage displays a distinctive bright green roof and dark green windowline. These are separated by a band of bright blue, with the lower section in white and the underside in grey. A white Shamrock is worn on the fin, and is repeated alongside the 'Aer Lingus' fuselage lettering in bright green. EI-ASJ, a Boeing 747-100, is seen here whilst on approach to London's Heathrow Airport. It was an unexpected visitor when it operated flight EI166 from Dublin on June 1 1988, replacing the usual Boeing 737-300. The company's Boeing ICAO call sign is 'SHAMROCK'. *(K.G. Wright)*

AEROLINEAS ARGENTINAS (AR/ARG)

Argentina

Aerolineas Argentinas was founded as a state corporation in May 1949, by the Ministry of Transport to take over the operations of Fama, Alfa, Aeroposta and Zarda. These companies finally ceased operations in December of that year, and were subsequently merged to form the Argentinean flag carrier. Today the airline operates an extensive network of scheduled passenger and cargo routes to points in North, South and Central America, New Zealand, the Far East, South Africa and Europe. International services radiate from Buenos Aires to Cape Town, Madrid, Rome, Zurich, Frankfurt, Paris (CDG), Los Angeles, Miami, New York (JFK), Montreal, Rio de Janeiro, Sao Paulo, Asuncion, Montevideo, La Paz, Caracas, Lima, Santiago, Guayaquil, Bogota, Porto Alegre, Mexico City, Hong Kong and Auckland. A fleet of Boeing 707, 727, 737, 747 and Fokker F-28 types is maintained. All aircraft utilized by Aerolineas Argentinas wear an identical livery which features twin cheatlines in medium and dark blue, extending from the nose, widening along the fuselage, and terminating on the fin, where each is topped by a similarly coloured 'A' initial. Dark blue 'Aerolineas Argentinas' titles are carried on the forward fuselage, as is the traditional bird logo, now a secondary feature of the scheme. Boeing 747SP-27, LV-OHV, can be seen here at Buenos Aires; the aircraft having just completed flight AR387 from Los Angeles. This 'SP' is in fact the company's sole example of this Boeing variant. It was purchased from Braniff International after that carrier had ceased trading. The aircraft had served with the United States company as N604BN, having been built in 1979. Aerolineas Argentinas' ICAO call sign is 'ARGENTINA'.
(K.G. Wright)

AIR CANADA (AC/ACA) Canada

Air Canada was formed on April 10 1937 as Trans Canada Airlines. The company's stock was held by Government-owned Canadian National Railways until February 1987, when the carrier became a Crown Corporation in its own right. Air Canada began operations between Vancouver and Seattle in 1938 and had established transcontinental passenger services by April 1939. The name of the airline was changed by Act of Parliament, from Trans Canada Airlines to Air Canada in 1965. In November 1987, the airline signed a letter of intent to purchase Northwest Territorial Airways. Through this investment, the company further extended its 'Air Canada Connector' feeder network. Currently participating in this operation are Air Nova (Air Canada purchased forty-nine per cent in 1986), Air BC (acquired in 1987), Air Ontario (formed by the merger of Austin Airways and Air Ontario in which the company has a seventy-five per cent holding), and Commuter Express. Air Canada operates an extensive network of scheduled passenger and cargo services within Canada, together with international routes to San Francisco, Los Angeles, Chicago, Tampa, Miami, New York (JFK), and Boston in the USA; Freeport, Nassau, Havana, Montego Bay, Kingston, Bermuda, Antigua, St. Lucia, Guadeloupe, Martinique,

Barbados, Haiti, Santo Domingo, Puerto Plata, and Port of Spain in the Caribbean; London (LHR), Manchester, Glasgow (PIK), Paris (CDG), Geneva, Zurich, Dusseldorf, Munich and Frankfurt in Europe. Scheduled services to Bombay and Singapore started in January 1985. After a ten-year gap, flights to Vienna were recommenced on April 26 1987. All-cargo flights operate to Brussels, London and Shannon. Charter services are also undertaken. A fleet of Boeing 727, 747, 767, DC-8, DC-9 and Lockheed L-1011 Tristar aircraft is maintained. An order for the Airbus A320 was placed in 1988; for delivery from 1990, replacing the Boeing 727 and DC-9 types. The current livery adopted by Air Canada, has been used since 1977. It features a warm red cheatline, a great deal more orange than the Canadian flag, and matching fin. The national Maple Leaf of Canada appears reversed out in a stylish form on the tail. Company titles are carried on the forward upper fuselage in warm red. C-GAGA, a Boeing 747-233B SCD, is seen here on departure from Heathrow Airport. The aircraft was operating flight AC857 to Toronto. The carrier's ICAO call sign is 'AIR CANADA'.
(B.T. Richards)

AIR CHINA (CA/CCA)

China

Air China, until recently known as CAAC, was formed on November 2 1949, after the founding of the People's Republic. Over the last two or three years, the company has been in the process of a major reorganisation. The aim was for the then CAAC, to concentrate increasingly on its role as a regulatory body and gradually to reduce its airline operations. In 1984 the national carrier, which was actually the Department of International Affairs within the Civil Aviation Administration of China, was broken up to create several regional carriers with varying degrees of independence. These include Air China, operating Beijing-based domestic and international routes; Shanghai (China Eastern Aviation); Guangzhou (China Southern Airlines); Chengdu (China Southwest Airlines); Fujia (Xiamen Airlines); Shenyang; Shenzen; Dalian (Northern Airlines), and Xianor-Langzhou (Northwest Airlines). Most of the airlines are heavily dependent on the Administration, but Shanghai has emerged as the first more independent carrier with scheduled services. The carrier's fleet consists of a mixture of western and eastern built types. These include Boeing 707, 737-200 and -300, 747, 767, A310, MD82, Trident, DHC-6, TU-154, IL-14, IL-18, AN-12, AN-

24, AN-26, BAe 146, Y-7, Li-2 and Shorts 360 aircraft. A wide range of varied helicopters is also utilized. Delivery of the Boeing 747-400 is awaited. The affiliated companies operate scheduled services on a rapidly expanding domestic network. Scheduled international services are operated to San Francisco, New York (JFK), Los Angeles, Bucharest, Frankfurt, Paris (CDG), Zurich, London (LGW), Rome, Addis Ababa, Belgrade, Sydney, Sharjah, Baghdad, Kuwait, Hong Kong, Singapore, Rangoon, Pyongyang, Moscow (SVO), Tokyo (NRT), Osaka, Nagasaki, Bangkok, Karachi and Manila. Air China's livery is dominated by a large national flag that appears on the tail with its leading edge always parallel to the fin. The white cabin roof and grey painted lower fuselage are separated by a narrow dark blue windowline that is trimmed above by a similarly coloured pin stripe. On some types the cheatline runs below window level. 'Air China' titles appear in black Chinese letters on both sides of the fuselage. B-2442, a Boeing 747SP-J6, seen at Gatwick Airport, operated flight CA937 from Beijing, via Sharjah and Zurich. The ICAO call sign is 'CHINA'. *(Flying Colours)*

AIR FRANCE (AF/AFR)   France

Air France was founded on August 30 1933, when Societe Centrale pour l'Exploitation De Lignes Aeriennes (formed shortly before, on May 19, by the merger of Air Orient, Air Union, Compagnie Internationale de Navigation Aerienne, and Societe Generale de Transport Aerien) purchased the assets of Compagnie Generale Aeropostale. After the Second World War air transport was nationalised and Societe Nationale Air France was set up on January 1 1946, followed by Compagnie Nationale Air France on June 16 1948, when the airline was incorporated by Act of Parliament. The flag carrier became one of the launch customers for the Airbus A340 in January 1987. It lost its monopoly on flights to the French overseas territories in 1986, when Minerve (see separate entry) and Point Air were licensed to operate charter flights alongside Air France's services. The state currently has a 99.38 per cent holding in the carrier. A comprehensive network covers an intricate pattern of medium haul routes throughout Europe, North Africa and the Middle East, and a long haul network extends to North and South America, the Caribbean Islands, Africa, Madagascar, and the Indian Ocean, China, Japan, and other points in the Far East. Air France also operates the French Postal Administration night mail services. Some European routes are operated by Transport Aerien Transregional (formerly known as Touraine Air Transport), as well as by Air Littoral, Britair, Europe Air and Air Limousin. The carrier is the only airline to operate to all of the United Kingdom's main and regional airports from its base at Paris (CDG). Air France operates a fleet of Concorde, Boeing 727, 737, 747, Airbus A300, A310, A320, Fokker F-27 and Transall types. When the present colourscheme was adopted in 1975, it was widely acclaimed as something totally new in airline livery design. A white overall fuselage finish is highlighted by blue 'Air France' fuselage titles and a very small horse logo, the famous 'Cleval Vapeur', in blue and red. The tail fin displays the major splash of colour in the form of blue and red stripes in varying widths. Pure-freight aircraft can be identified by additional 'Cargo' titling alongside the company name. This is however, separated from the main lettering by a 'Flying Pelican'. F-GPAN, a Boeing 747-2B3F SCD, is seen here at Paris (CDG). The carrier's ICAO call sign is 'AIR FRANCE'. *(K.G. Wright)*

AIR LANKA (UL/ALK)   Sri Lanka

Air Lanka, the national flag carrier of Sri Lanka, was formed on January 10 1979 to succeed the defunct Air Ceylon. Major shareholder is the Government, with sixty per cent; the remaining forty per cent lying in the hands of public companies in Sri Lanka, including the Ceylon Shipping Company and the Bank of Ceylon. Scheduled passenger and cargo operations from Katunayke International Airport, Colombo, began on September 1 1979. These now link Sri Lanka with Bangkok, Singapore, Hong Kong, Kuala Lumpur, Tokyo (NRT), Tiruchirapaly, Trivandrum, Madras, Bombay, Male, Frankfurt, Amsterdam and London (LGW). Subsidiaries include Air Lanka Catering Services, a joint venture with Thai International. The company's colourscheme starts with a bright red windowline that runs from the nose and eventually encompasses the entire tail,

forming the backdrop for the airline's large white Peacock motif. The whole fuselage is finished in white with black 'Air Lanka' titles, alongside a representation of the Sri Lankan flag. The carrier's fleet consists of Boeing 737 and Lockheed L-1011 Tristar aircraft. Air Lanka no longer operates its two Boeing 747-238Bs. These were originally purchased from Qantas as 4R-ULF and 4R-ULG, ex VH-EBA and VH-EBB, respectively. These have now been returned to the Australian carrier and have since taken up their original registrations. 4R-ULF, 'King Vijaya', can be seen here at Sydney Airport during engine runs, prior to its first flight for Air Lanka, on June 4 1984. The carrier's ICAO call sign is 'AIR LANKA'.
(Author's Collection)

AIR MADAGASCAR (MD/MDG)

Madagascar

Air Madagascar, the national carrier of the Malagasy Republic, is 80.64 per cent owned by the Government and 19.36 per cent by Air France and La Compagnie Generale Maritime. The company was formed on January 1 1962 by the Government of the newly founded Malagasy Republic, and Air France. Today, the carrier has various subsidiaries that include the SOMHI hotel complex, the ZAHA motel chain, the tour organiser Malagasy Airtours, Casino Club, Sofitrans, ARSATO and TAM. For such a small country, Air Madagascar's fleet is comparatively large in size. With a fleet of Piper PA31, Cessna 402B, BAe 748, DHC-6 Twin Otter, Boeing 737 and 747 aircraft, the airline flies to a number of destinations. With a base at Antananarivo, flights are maintained to Zurich, Paris (ORY), and Marseilles, via Djibouti. Services are also flown to Nairobi, Mauritius, Reunion, Dar Es Salaam, Jeddah and the Comores Islands. A domestic network links the Madagascan capital with Ambanjo, Ambatomainty,

Ambatndrzka, Andriamena, Ankavandra, Antalaha, Antsalova, Antsiranana, Antsohihy, Bealanana, Belo, Farafangana, Fianarantsoa, Fort Dauphin, Maintirano, Majunga, Manakara, Mananara, Mananjary, Maroantsetra, Miandrivazo, Morafenobe, Morondava, Nossi-Be, Saint Marie, Sambava, Tamatave, Tsaratanana, Tsiroanomandi, and Tulear. Air Madagascar's livery utilizes a brick red cheatline which disects an all-white fuselage; and is trimmed by a narrower stripe in the same colour. The national flag is displayed halfway along the cabin roof, quite a way from the bold green 'Air Madagascar' titling on the forward upper fuselage. The tail fin is dominated by a flying bird of prey in brick red, passing a green stylised tree. 5R-MFT, the company's sole Boeing 747-2B2B, can be seen here. The aircraft is named 'Tolom Piavotana'. Air Madagascar's ICAO call sign is 'MADAIR'. *(Flying Colours)*

AIR MALAWI (QM/AML)

Malawi

Air Malawi, the national flag carrier, was formed in 1964 as a wholly-owned subsidiary of Central African Airways, to fly local services within the newly independent Republic of Malawi, formerly Nyasaland. Following the dissolution of CAA in mid-1967, the carrier separated entirely from its former partners and was established in its own right on September 1 of that year. Today the airline is owned by the Malawi Government and operates a network of regional services from the capital, Blantyre, to Harare, Beira, Mauritius, Johannesburg, Nairobi and Lusaka. Domestic flights are maintained to Lilongwe, Mzuzu, Mangochi and Karonga. Charter operations are also maintained in the northern region. A fleet of Beechcraft King Air, Shorts Skyvan, BAe 1-11 and BAe 748 aircraft is maintained. Although no longer operated, the Boeing 747SP-44 depicted here, 7Q-YKL, was leased from South African Airways during the early part of 1985 to transport the President of Malawi on his state visit to the United Kingdom. The aircraft remained dormant at London's Heathrow Airport for the entire duration of the head of state's stay. It should be noted that the Boeing aircraft was subsequently returned to SAA as ZS-SPB, before being leased to Luxair (see separate entry). The Air Malawi cheatline, which widens gradually as it progresses along the cabin, is coloured to represent the national flag, in black, red and green. Red company titles in lower case lettering, are worn centrally, on the roof. Again, red is the dominant colour, this time it covers the entire fin. This displays the company motif, of a white 'M' initial which rides on the back of a stylised bird; that flies across a red sun, and is repeated alongside the main passenger door. It should be noted that the leased Boeing 747SP wore the standard tail design and lettering of Air Malawi, but retained the 'straight through' midnight blue cheatline of South African Airways. The carrier's ICAO call sign is 'MALAWI'.

(K.C. Wright)

AIR MAURITIUS
(MK/MAU)

Mauritius

Air Mauritius was originally formed on June 14 1967 as a multi national venture between the Mauritian Government, BOAC, Rogers & Co., and Air France; with Air India joining at a later date. It was not until August 1972 that services finally commenced, when a single Piper Navajo was leased for a flight to Rodrigues. Today, major shareholders are the Government of Mauritius (fifty-one per cent), Rogers & Co. (14.94 per cent), British Airways Associated Companies (12.77 per cent), and Air India (8.52 per cent). Scheduled passenger and cargo services link Plaisance International Airport with Nairobi, Zurich, Munich, Geneva, Rome, Paris (ORY), London (LHR), Antananarivo, Reunion, Bombay, Johannesburg, Durban, Moroni, Singapore, and the adjacent island of Rodrigues. Commuter flights also link the capital with other neighbouring islands. For quite a number of years, Air Mauritius's fleet consisted of DHC-6 Twin Otters for local services, and a Boeing 707, leased in from British Airways. The latter type has since been replaced, due to noise regulations, and today a fleet of Boeing 747SP (leased from South African Airways), Boeing 767, DHC-6, ATR-42, and Bell 206B Jetranger II aircraft is utilized. Air Mauritius's colourscheme is bold and representative. The fuselage, white down to wing level, sports an attractive bright red windowline that is trimmed below with a similarly coloured pinstripe. Bold upper case red 'Air Mauritius' titles adorn the forward fuselage, alongside the national flag. A bright red Falcon 'hovers' on the tail, within a white band across a predominantly red fin. The livery worn by the DHC-6 types differs slightly by displaying 'Air Mauritius' titles between the cheatlines, which are set wider apart to accommodate them. The carrier's ICAO call sign is 'AIR MAURITIUS'. *(K.G. Wright)*

AIR NEW ZEALAND
(NZ & TE/ANZ)

New Zealand

The national carrier of New Zealand was founded as Tasman Empire Airways, a joint British-Australian-New Zealand company (owned 20:30:50), formed to operate services linking New Zealand and Australia. In 1954 Britain withdrew, and in 1961 the New Zealand Government assumed full ownership of the airline which, on April 1 1965, adopted the present title. In 1977 the Government decided to merge the two state-owned domestic and international airlines. From April 1 1978, New Zealand National Airways and Air New Zealand were amalgamated under the latter name. NZNAC was formed in 1945, beginning operations two years later. Associated companies of Air New Zealand include Safe Air (100 per cent holding) and Instant Freeline Reservations. The airline also has a seventy-seven per cent stake in the Mount Cook Group, as well as a fifty per cent holding in Jetset Tours. The company operates an extensive network of scheduled passenger and cargo services to twenty-four main domestic points, while international routes link Auckland, Christchurch and Wellington with Sydney, Melbourne,

Perth, Brisbane, Hobart, Hong Kong, Singapore, Tokyo (NRT), Nadi, Tonga, Apia, Noumea, Norfolk Island, Raratonga, Papeete, Honolulu, Los Angeles, Dallas/Ft. Worth, Vancouver, Frankfurt and London (LGW). A fleet of Boeing 737, 747, 767 and Fokker F-27 types is maintained. An order for the Boeing 747-400 is outstanding. It was decided that the old Air New Zealand livery, introduced in 1973, over five years prior to the merger, would be retained in preference to the orange and red of NZNAC. It is this scheme that appears on all aircraft fleetwide. Twin 'straight through' cheatlines in deep blue and turquoise underline blue 'Air New Zealand' roof titling which appear in a bold typeface, alongside the national flag. This refined colour combination, evoking images of the Pacific, is repeated on the fin to form the backdrop for a traditional Maori symbol, known as a 'Koru'. ZK-NZY, a Boeing 747-219B, is seen here at Honolulu International Airport. It was operating flight TE6 from Auckland, via Nadi. The carrier's ICAO call sign is 'NEW ZEALAND'.
(Author's Collection)

AIR PACIFIC (FJ/FJI)

Fiji

Air Pacific, the flag carrier of Fiji, was incorporated on April 13 1947 as Katoflanga Estates Limited. In 1951 the company changed its name to Fiji Airways, and operated its first services in September of that year, using de Havilland Dragon Rapide equipment. By 1957 Qantas, the Australian national airline, had purchased the company, and subsequently opened international services on its behalf. Towards the end of the 1960s, several Pacific islands had joined the Fijian Government, Air New Zealand, BOAC and Qantas as major shareholders. In 1971 a second name change was made to the present title, and by the end of 1978 the Government had purchased all of the other airline shares to hold the majority shareholding. Today Air Pacific maintains a wide network of scheduled passenger services. Flights are operated to New Zealand, Australia, New Caledonia, Tonga, Western Samoa, Tahiti, the Solomon Islands and Vanuatu. In addition a regional network is maintained as well as services within the Fijian Islands. A fleet of ATR-42, Boeing 737 and 747 aircraft is maintained. The latter type of which is used, in conjunction with Qantas, on the Nadi-Honolulu-Los Angeles long haul route. Air Pacific's colourscheme must be one of the most colourful ever applied to an airline fleet, especially in this case, the 747. A white forward half of the fuselage contrasts with bands of yellow, orange, magenta and a deep blue; the latter engulfing the entire vertical fin. The stylish company motif of a blue, yellow, orange and magenta rainbow, behind a leaping Merlin, is displayed across the tail. Dark blue 'Air Pacific' titles adorn the forward fuselage. The Boeing 747-238B depicted here, VH-EBK, has since been returned to Qantas. Several aircraft from that company's fleet have replaced this unit, at one time or another. The most current example being VH-EEI, a Series 100, having previously served with the short-lived Scottish airline, Highland Express, as G-HIHO. The carrier's ICAO call sign is 'PACIFIC'. *(Flying Colours)*

ALITALIA (AZ/AZA) Italy

Alitalia, the national carrier of Italy, was formed in September 1946 under the name, Aerolinee Italiene Internationali, in conjunction with British European Airways. Its aim was to operate converted war-surplus bombers over a domestic passenger network. 1948 saw the first international flight to Buenos Aires. The present title was adopted in October 1957, when the company was merged with Linee Aeree Italiene. An extensive worldwide network of scheduled passenger and cargo services is operated from Italy to points in Europe, Africa, North and South America, the Middle and Far East, and Australia. Some recent highlights have included the joint launch with CAAC in July 1986 of a Beijing-Rome (via Sharjah) service, initially using the latter company's aircraft. In October of that year Alitalia launched flights to Lima, in Peru. The company colour-scheme, designed by Walter Landor Associates, was created to take the carrier into the seventies. It was regarded by many to be the most modern of its time, and still ranks amongst the most attractive. The livery's centrepiece is a stylised 'A' logo in green, with a red centre. It is formed on the tail as a continuation of the basic green windowline and is repeated within the black 'Alitalia' fuselage lettering, in black and red. It should be noted that small 'Alitalia' titles in gold on the cheatline appear alongside each passenger door, and that the fuselage base colour is white on all aircraft throughout the fleet. The engine cowlings are in natural metal, with the exception of the MD82s, which are painted grey. Alitalia operates a fleet of Boeing 747, DC-9, MD82, A300, Piaggio P166-DL3, and SIAI Marchetti SF-260 aircraft. An order for the MD11 is currently outstanding. I-DEML, a 747-200, is seen here at New York's JFK International, having operated flight AZ1600 from Rome, via Milan. The carrier's ICAO call sign is 'ALITALIA'.

(K.G. Wright)

ALL NIPPON AIRWAYS (NH/ANA)

Japan

All Nippon Airways was formed in December 1952 as the Japan Helicopter and Airplane Company, with scheduled services beginning in 1953. Over the next few years JHAT grew in size and strength, with the merger between itself and Far Eastern Airlines in 1958. This was followed by a take-over of Fujita Airlines in 1963, Nakanihon Air Services in 1965, and Nagasaki Airways in 1967. Today All Nippon Airlines ranks as one of Japan's major airlines. The company launched its first scheduled international passenger service in March 1986. This linked Tokyo (NRT) with Guam. Tokyo (NRT)-Los Angeles, Tokyo (NRT)-Washington (IAD) and Tokyo (NRT)-Hong Kong were added in July of that year, Tokyo (NRT)-Sydney was added not long afterwards. In April 1987, ANA inaugurated scheduled services to Beijing, with Seoul being added on July 1 1988. The route to London (LGW) received approval in Spring 1989. The carrier has around 115,000 shareholders, of which the largest is the Nagoya Railroad (five per cent). In addition to its international scheduled services, ANA operates scheduled passenger and cargo services to over seventy domestic and regional points, as well as maintaining a limited number of shorthaul charter services. A fleet of L-1011 Tristar, Boeing 727, 737, 747, 767, YS-11

and AS350B Ecureuil aircraft is maintained. Delivery of Boeing 747-400 and Airbus A320-200 types will begin during the 1990s. All Nippon Airways is part of the ANA Group, which has over one hundred companies in its midst. These include, ANA Enterprises, ANA Trading, ANA World Tours, and ANA Information Systems Planning. Finally, there is Nippon Cargo Airlines, (see separate entry). The year 1983 saw the dawn of a new era when All Nippon introduced a stylish new livery to coincide with the delivery of the company's first Boeing 767. An angled cheatline arrangement, in two new shades of blue, was chosen to replace the pale blue scheme that had been worn for many years. 'All Nippon Airways' titling in Japanese and English appears on either side of the fuselage, alongside the national flag. Large 'ANA' letters in English dominates the tail fin in white. This replaces the traditional Leonardo da Vinci helicopter motif. The carrier's ICAO call sign is 'ALL NIPPON'. JA8175, a Boeing 747-281B, is seen here at Washington's Dulles Airport, having operated flight NH002 from Tokyo. *(U. Schaefer Collection)*

AMERICAN AIRLINES (AA/AAL)

United States of America

American Airlines, the huge Texan-based carrier, was founded in 1934 as a direct successor to American Airways; itself formed in January 1930 through the merger of several small companies. The carrier is today one of the world's largest airlines, having acquired Air Cal in 1986, and absorbed the company's operations in 1987. In 1986 American commenced a major development of five new hubs at Dallas, Chicago, Raleigh/Durham, Nashville and San Juan. An extensive network of feeder routes are operated under the name 'American Eagle', utilizing the services of a number of regional and commuter airlines. American's network of scheduled passenger and cargo services extends from the Atlantic coast to Hawaii, as well as to Toronto and Montreal in the north and Mexico City, Acapulco, Guadalajara, Cancun, Cozumel, and Puerto Vallarta to the south. In 1971 the airline absorbed Trans Caribbean Airways and began flying to Puerto Rico, the US Virgin Islands (as American Inter Island), Aruba, Curacao, and Haiti. American started services to Bermuda, Barbados, and Santo Domingo in 1975, through a route exchange with Pan Am. The airline flies to Jamaica and other Caribbean points. American commenced services from Dallas to London (LGW) in May 1982, and introduced services to Paris (ORY), Manchester, Dusseldorf and Munich in 1986. Flights from Chicago to Zurich and Geneva were added in 1987. The carrier also introduced transpacific services that same year, flying from Dallas/Ft. Worth and Houston to Tokyo (NRT). A fleet of Boeing 727, 737, 747SP, 767, MD82, MD83, DC-10, BAe 146 and A300 aircraft is maintained. Delivery of Boeing 757s is eagerly anticipated. The current livery, although still appearing modern, was introduced in 1969 to take the company into the seventies. A highly polished fuselage and tail are the order of the day. It should be noted however, that some aircraft types, namely the A300, Boeing 737 and 747SP sport a grey tail. Either way, it provides an excellent backdrop for a patriotic triple cheatline in red, white and blue, whilst 'American' lettering in red, outlined in white, is displayed on the cabin roof. The tail fin hosts the traditional company motif of a blue eagle swooping down between the peaks of the double 'A' initials. The ICAO call sign is 'AMERICAN'. *(U. Schaefer Collection)*

AVIANCA COLOMBIA (AV/AVA)

Colombia

Avianca, Colombia's national carrier, has the distinction of being the oldest airline in the Americas. The company can trace its history back to 1919, when its predecessor, SCADTA was formed by five Colombian and three German businessmen. In 1931 Pan American acquired an eighty per cent shareholding. Nine years later the present title was adopted when SCADTA merged with Servicio Aero Colombiano. 1954 saw Avianca take over the domestic carrier, SAETA; and by 1978, the company had bought outright Pan Am's original shareholding. Wholly-owned subsidiaries are Sociedade Aeronautica de Medellin (SAM), and Helicol. Today Avianca, based at Bogota's Eldorado Airport, operates an extensive domestic network, together with routes to Madrid, Paris (CDG) and Frankfurt in Europe; to Miami, New York (JFK), Los Angeles, Panama City, Mexico City and San Juan, Curacao, Aruba, Port-au-Prince, and Santo Domingo in North and Central America; as well as to Quito, Lima, Santiago, Buenos Aires, Rio de Janeiro, Caracas, and Montevideo in South America. The company maintains an all-Boeing fleet of 707, 727, 747 and 767 aircraft types. It is anticipated that Avianca will commence scheduled services to London (LGW) using its 767s. During July and August 1988, the carrier operated several flights into the British airport, using Boeing 707s; however, these were only on a charter basis. The company's livery is bright and somewhat distinctive with the fuselage being painted in a warm red, in a 'dolphin' style unique to Avianca and Iraqi Airways. This is designed to streamline the aircraft's overall appearance. 'Avianca Colombia' titles adorn the upper forward fuselage in white and black respectively, and the tail livery, redesigned in the early eighties, features red 'Avianca' lettering, which is underlined by a continuation of the fuselage cheatlines which colour the rear half of the fin. HK-2980X, a Boeing 747-259B SCD, is seen on arrival at Frankfurt Main Airport. The aircraft, operating flight AV010 from Bogota, via Caracas, Madrid and Paris (CDG), is leased-in to the carrier from the Chemco Leasing Company. The airline's ICAO call sign is 'AVIANCA'. *(K.G. Wright)*

BRITISH AIRWAYS (BA-BAW)

United Kingdom

British Airways was formed in September 1972, following the merger of British Overseas Airways Corporation (founded in 1940), BOAC Associated Companies, BOAC Engine Overhauls, British European Airways Corporation (founded in 1946), BEA Airtours, BEA Helicopters, Northeast Airlines, Cambrian Airways, and International Aeradio. Formally integrated operations began on April 1 1974, and the airline was further rationalized into a single unified operating structure in April 1977. Just under ten years later, British Airways was privatised. In December 1987 the airline acquired British Caledonian Airways and all its assets. The new and enlarged British Airways, and its charter subsidiary, Caledonian Airways, operates an extensive network of routes. Scheduled and charter passenger and freight services are maintained throughout the United Kingdom to major cities in Europe, the Middle and Far East, Australia, New Zealand, Africa, North and South America. A fleet of Concorde, Boeing 737, 747, 757, 767, L-1011 Tristar, BAe 1-11, BAe 748 and BAe ATP aircraft is utilized. A large order for the Boeing 747-400 is outstanding, as is one for the MD11, which British Airways has accepted as part of the take-over deal of British

Caledonian. All of the latter type however, will be leased out to various airlines, following an agreement with aircraft leasing giant, Guinness Peat Aviation. The airline colourscheme was officially unveiled on December 4 1984, becoming the first major livery change for the company for over a decade. Landor Associates were the creators of the new image, which retained the former midnight blue lower fuselage for identification when airborne, and features a new red 'Speedwing', which runs the length of the fuselage. This gives an added touch of colour. The top half of the fin is royal blue, and displays a pearl grey coat of arms above a quartered Union Flag. The whole of the upper fuselage is in pearl grey, thus promoting the new style midnight blue 'British Airways' lettering. All aircraft in the fleet wear this livery, with the exception of Concorde, which is unique in that it must always be painted predominantly white for heat reflection purposes. A Boeing 747-200, seen here en route to Nairobi, depicts the outstanding livery. The carrier's ICAO call sign is 'SPEEDBIRD', but when Shuttle flights are operated, the 'SHUTTLE' sign is used. *(British Airways)*

C.A.L. CARGO AIRLINES (ICL)

Israel

C.A.L. Cargo Airlines was formed in June 1986 as a joint venture by a number of the country's major importers and exporters. Operations did not however, start until November 1 of that year. Today, the airline operates freight charter flights from Tel Aviv to cities in Western Europe and the USA. These include London (LHR), Cologne, Amsterdam, Paris (CDG), Brussels, Rome, Zurich and Los Angeles. Primary cargo is perishable agricultural goods, however, general charter flights are undertaken. Shareholders of the company are the Jewish Labour Settlement (fifty-six per cent), the Production and Marketing Board of Ornamental Plants (eighteen per cent), the Vegetable Marketing Board (eighteen per cent) and the Fruit Board of Israel (eight per cent). Boeing 747 freighters are leased in, as and when required from the national flag carrier, EL AL. Although

C.A.L. has an official company livery, this has, as yet, never been applied to an aircraft. The colourscheme features an arrowhead in four shades of blue, black titles and brown cheatline with matching box motif. All aircraft currently operate in a basic two-tone scheme of the owner, EL AL. However, all titles have been removed and replaced by basic C.A.L. lettering in white on the fin, and deep blue on the fuselage. 4X-AXZ, a Boeing 747-124 SCD (converted to a freighter), is seen here on departure from London's Heathrow Airport, for its flight to Tel Aviv, via Amsterdam. It should be noted that this aircraft disregards the colourscheme by only wearing red 'Cargo' titles in upper case letters on the forward fuselage. The carrier's ICAO call sign is 'CAL'. *(B.T. Richards)*

CARGOLUX AIRLINES INTERNATIONAL (CV/CLX)

Luxembourg

Cargolux, Europe's largest all-cargo airline, was formed in March 1970 by Loftleider SA and Luxair, the Grand Duchy of Luxembourg's flag carrier. Regular cargo flights are operated to the Middle and Far East, and to the USA (Seattle, San Francisco, Miami, Houston, and New York (JFK)), as well as worldwide charter flights, maintenance, and sub leasing services. The company's operational base is at Luxembourg's Findel Airport, from where an extensive trucking network is operated to various European cities. Shareholders are Flugleider Icelandair, Salen Shipping, Luxair, and a group of Luxembourg interests, the latter of which hold a majority stake. A fleet of three Boeing 747-271C (SCD) aircraft is maintained. In 1987 Cargolux and Luxair formed a passenger-carrying company, Lionair (see separate entry); two Boeing 747-121 types are utilized.

The national flag of Luxembourg is portrayed in the colourscheme by twin cheatlines of bright red and blue, divided by a narrow white stripe. This extends along the entire length of the aircraft over a pale grey painted fuselage. It should be noted that until January 1985, the base colour was a highly polished natural metal, although the remainder of the livery, including the grey painted tail, was the same as that currently worn. Bold 'Cargolux' titles in black lower case lettering interrupts the cheatline on the forward fuselage, and the grey tail sports the company's 'triple box' motif in outlined red. LX-DCV, a Boeing 747-2R7F, can be seen here after its arrival at Miami Airport. It should be noted that this particular aircraft is no longer with the company. The carrier's ICAO call sign is 'CARGOLUX'. *(U. Schaefer Collection)*

CATHAY PACIFIC (CX/CPX)

Hong Kong

Cathay Pacific, founded in September 1946, initially operated a fleet of several war-surplus Douglas DC-3s. These were used on freight and, later, passenger services on a route network which stretched from Shanghai to Sydney. Since 1948 the airline has been controlled and managed by the Swire Group. Following increases, and a subsequent reorganization of share capital between 1970 and 1975, and the purchase in 1980 of a fifteen per cent shareholding from British Airways Associated Companies, Cathay Holdings took over 70 per cent of the issued capital. Today, Hong Kong's flag carrier operates an extensive network of scheduled passenger and cargo services from Hong Kong to Abu Dhabi, Amsterdam, Auckland, Bahrain, Bandar Seri Begawan, Bangkok, Beijing, Bombay, Brisbane, Denpasar, Dhahran, Dubai, Frankfurt, Fukuoka, Jakarta, Kaosiung, Kota Kinabalu, Kuala Lumpur, London (LGW), Manila, Melbourne, Nagoya, Osaka, Paris (ORY), Penang, Perth, Rome, San Francisco, Seoul, Shanghai, Singapore, Sydney, Taipei (CKS), Tokyo (NRT) and Vancouver. Major shareholders are Swire Pacific (50.2 per cent),

the Hong Kong and Shanghai Banking Corporation (16.4 per cent), and China International Trust and Investment Corporation (12.5 per cent). The company is listed on the Hong Kong stock exchange. Cathay Pacific maintains a fleet of Boeing 747 and L-1011 Tristar aircraft. An order for the Boeing 747-400 is outstanding. A subtle shade of medium green was chosen to colour the broad, classically-styled, cheatline, which widens at the front and is trimmed below in white. The all-green fin displays two streamline white bands that run below a small Union flag, but is otherwise devoid of company motif. Bold red 'Cathay Pacific' titling appears alongside the Swire Group's motif on the upper forward fuselage. The all-freight Boeing 747s can be identified by red 'cargo' lettering between the Swire Group flag and the usual titling, in a similar script. VR-HVZ, a Boeing 747-236F SCD, can be seen here at Frankfurt Main in October 1987. The company's ICAO call sign is 'CATHAY'.
(B.T. Richards)

CHINA AIRLINES (CI/CAL) Taiwan

China Airlines was formed in December 1959, its purpose being to provide charter services utilizing two former military Catalina Flying Boats. The company was made the official flag carrier of the Republic of China in 1965. Since that year, China Airlines has rapidly expanded its international services. From a base at Taipei's Chiang Kai Shek International airport, the airline flies to Amsterdam, Anchorage, Bangkok, Dhahran, Fukuoka, Hong Kong, Honolulu, Jakarta, Kuala Lumpur, Los Angeles, Manila, New York (JFK), Okinawa, San Francisco, Seoul, Singapore and Tokyo (NRT). CAL also flies to several points within Taiwan. Up until 1987, the carrier had the distinction of being one of the only scheduled passenger-carrying airlines to fly around the world. This was lost when it dropped its New York to Amsterdam route, due to poor load factors. Also removed were the European cities of Frankfurt and Vienna. China Airlines also operates an extensive network of cargo services. The fleet is made up almost entirely of wide-bodied aircraft, the exception being three Boeing 737-200 types, which are utilized on domestic scheduled services. The long-haul sectors are served by Airbus A300B4 and -600, Boeing 747-200, Boeing 747SP

and Boeing 767 types. An order for six Boeing 747-400s is currently outstanding. CAL was the first airline in the world to operate the A300 and Boeing 767 together. It was also the first company in Asia to purchase the latter type. As with the majority of national carriers, China Airlines' aircraft sport patriotic colours. In this instance these being red, white and blue. The basic cheatline is repeated vertically up the tail which is without company motif. Instead, it displays the Taiwanese flag above the registration number. Fuselage titling in blue reads 'China Airlines' in English, with its Chinese equivalent on the starboard. This is reversed on the port. It should also be noted that the registration is also carried on the forward lower fuselage, and that 737s, 767s and A300s sport grey undersides. The pure-freight aircraft sports large 'Dynasty Cargo' lettering in both languages flanking the company motif. The latter not being used in the normal company livery. Boeing 747SP-09, N4508H, is seen here on arrival at Amsterdam's Schipol Airport. The aircraft was operating as flight number CI061, via Bangkok and Dhahran.
(K.C. Wright)

CONDOR FLUGDIENST (DF/CFG)

Federal Republic of Germany

Condor was formed in October 1961 by the merger of Deutsche Flugdienst (founded in 1955 as a Lufthansa subsidiary) and Condor Luftreederei (founded in 1957 and acquired by Lufthansa in 1959). Today the company is regarded as one of the world's largest charter airlines, operating intercontinental tour and general passenger group flights with an all-jet fleet of aircraft. Regular tour charter services are operated from Frankfurt, Dusseldorf, Munich and Stuttgart. Other German gateways include Hamburg, Bremen, Hannover and Saarbrucken. Condor operates package tour flights to destinations in Spain, Greece, the Canary Islands, Italy, Portugal, Turkey, Tunisia, Morocco, Kenya, Thailand, Sri Lanka, the United States, Canada, and Mexico. An emphasis is given to a very high quality of service, which the airline prides itself upon. A fleet of Airbus A310, Boeing 727, 737 and Douglas DC-10 aircraft is operated with several examples of the Boeing 757 on order. In the early 1970s, Condor purchased two Boeing 747-230B types. D-ABYF 'Fritz', was

delivered on April 20 1971, whilst D-ABYH 'Max', arrived on April 7 1972. For nearly seven years, these aircraft flew long haul, and high capacity routes; and were also the airline's flagships. In 1979, due to low passenger loads, the 747s were sold. Condor's livery was originally designed with tasteful practicality in mind. Unfortunately however, a design change was necessary, following delivery of the company's first Airbus A310. This was done through the re-painting of the otherwise natural metal fuselage, to a distinctive overall pale grey, which has now been adopted fleetwide. A lemon yellow fin adds the necessary touch of colour and displays a styled encircled flying Condor bird motif in a deep blue. This has been repeated under the cockpit windows and on each engine cowling; which is complemented by bold 'Condor' titles in a deep blue, near the forward passenger door. The carrier's ICAO call sign is 'CONDOR'. One of the company's two Boeing 747s can be seen here in the mid-seventies, sporting the airline's original livery. *(Flying Colours)*

CONTINENTAL AIRLINES (CO/COA)

United States of America

Continental Airlines, owned by the Texas Air Corporation, made a rapid expansion between 1986 and 1987, when it acquired the People Express Group. This consisted of Frontier Airlines, People Express, Britt Airways and Provincetown Boston Airlines. The company can trace its history back to 1934, when it began services as Varney Speed Lines. In May 1937 it purchased the Denver to Pueblo route of Wyoming Air Service and moved its headquarters to Denver. Later the same year, the name Continental Airlines was adopted. Development continued until the 1955 award of the Chicago to Los Angeles route (via Kansas City and Denver), which marked the company's full transition to a mainline trunk carrier. In October 1981 Texas Air, parent company of Texas International Airlines, acquired a controlling interest in Continental, and on October 31 1982, after several months of operating co-ordinated schedules, the two started to operate as a single carrier under the name of Continental. In September 1983, due to catastrophic losses, the company filed for protection under Chapter 11 bankruptcy. As a result of this the airline's domestic network was reduced from seventy-eight points to twenty-five, and its workforce declined from

12,000 to 4,200. Three years later, after a dramatic improvement in finances, Continental emerged from bankruptcy. Today the airline operates from its base in Houston, Texas to seventy-nine cities across the USA. International lines are maintained to the UK, France, New Zealand, Fiji, Australia, Venezuela and Mexico. The carrier's livery has changed very little since its introduction in 1968, apart from the tail motif which has recently been re-allied fleetwide in a bright red, instead of the original black. The cheatline consists of three colours, gold, red and orange, although the lower colours have blended, thus giving the appearance of solid cheatlines. Black 'Continental' titles adorn the cabin roof, having been enlarged during the recent facelift. The registration was previously reversed-out of the lower cheatline at the rear in white, although some fleet members show it below the cheatline in red alongside the national flag, which has been removed from the cabin roof. Continental's fleet consists of Boeing 727, 737, 747, DC-9, DC-10, MD-82 and A300 types. A Boeing 747-200 is seen here at Gatwick, after arrival from Miami as C030. The ICAO call sign is 'CONTINENTAL'. *(K.G. Wright)*

EGYPTAIR (MS/EGY)   Egypt

Egyptair was formed in May 1932 as Misr Airwork, and commenced services the following year. In 1949 the company became completely Egyptian-owned and the name was changed to Misrair SAE. By 1960 the airline had been renamed United Arab Airlines. October 10 1971 saw a final name change to Egyptair. It was announced in November 1980 that the carrier was to be financially reorganised and the share capital was to be held equally by the National Bank of Egypt and Misr Insurance. Today, the airline operates international scheduled passenger services to Athens, Brussels, Copenhagen, Dusseldorf, Frankfurt, Geneva, Larnaca, London (LHR), Madrid, Milan, Munich, Paris (ORY), Rhodes, Rome, Vienna and Zurich in Europe; Abu Dhabi, Amman, Baghdad, Bahrain, Dhahran, Doha, Dubai, Jeddah, Kuwait, Muscat, Sana'a and Sharjah in the Middle East; Algiers, Abidjan, Accra, Dar-es-Salaam, Kano, Khartoum, Lagos, Nairobi and Tunis in Africa; and Bangkok, Bombay, Karachi, Manila and Tokyo (NRT) in the Far East. Domestic services are operated under the name of Misrair. Egyptair operates a fleet of Boeing 707, 737, 747, 767 and Airbus A300 aircraft. The airline's colourscheme starts off with Horus, the omnipotent Falcon-headed god of ancient Egypt, appearing in red and black, within a gold disk, on the tail fin. This is repeated on the engines. A broad windowline takes its colour from the Egyptian flag and runs from nose to tail above a narrower line in gold. Black 'Egyptair' titling in both English and Arabic, separated by the Egyptian flag, appears on the forward upper fuselage. Boeing 767s display a highly-polished lower fuselage but this is left natural metal or grey on other types. Boeing 747-269B SCD, 9K-ADA, is seen here wearing full Egyptair colours, despite the fact that it was, at the time, on an operational lease from Kuwait Airways. This contract ended in June 1988 and the aircraft was back in its owner's livery on July 27 of that year. The aircraft is seen at Paris (ORY) whilst being towed to the terminal to await passengers for its flight MS986 to Cairo. Now that the company's two Boeing 747-300 Combi aircraft have been delivered, it should be noted that these now wear a slightly revised livery. The cheatline now runs on up the tail, stops beneath the 'head of Horus', and then continues through to the tip of the fin. The company's ICAO call sign is 'EGYPTAIR'. *(K.G. Wright)*

EL AL ISRAEL AIRLINES (LY/ELY)

Israel

EL AL was founded in November 1948 as the national flag carrier of the newly formed state of Israel. Scheduled services to Europe were initiated the following year, using Douglas DC-4 aircraft. Flights to the USA and South Africa were added in 1950. Today the majority shareholder is the Israeli Government, with the Jewish Agency, Histradut (the General Federation of Labour), and the Zim Israel Shipping Company also having an interest. Subsidiaries are Sun D'Or (formerly EL AL Charter Services), Teshat (partners on Laromme Hotels), and Tamam (in-flight catering services). A fleet of Boeing 707, 747, 757 and 767 aircraft is maintained over a scheduled passenger and cargo route network that links Tel Aviv with Amsterdam, Athens, Brussels, Bucharest, Cairo, Cologne, Copenhagen, London (LHR), Manchester, Marseille, Lisbon, Madrid, Istanbul, Munich, Paris (ORY), Rome, Vienna, Zurich, Geneva and Frankfurt. Flights also serve Nairobi, Johannesburg, New York (JFK), Montreal, Miami, Chicago, Los Angeles and Boston. A service between Elat and London (LHR) is also maintained. Negotiations are taking place with Thai International for a weekly service to Bangkok, via Nairobi; equipment will either be the Boeing 747 or 767, depending on the outcome of talks. The airline hopes that the first service will take place sometime towards the end of 1989. The company colour-scheme commences with a white fuselage. This is disected by an unusual windowlevel cheatline arrangement which is coloured a bright blue with a diagonal wedge. The upper rear fuselage continues this colouring and extends upwards to encompass most of the tail fin, which is topped by the Israeli flag. Dual language titles appear on the forward fuselage with 'EL AL' in black English lettering, intermingled with the Hebrew equivalent in gold. All aircraft in the fleet are adorned in a similar livery, however it should be noted that on the Boeing 747s, the cheatline continues on to the nose radome, but on other types it commences with a wedge under the cockpit windows. The company's ICAO call sign is 'EL AL'.

(K.G. Wright)

GARUDA INDONESIA (GA/GIA)

Indonesia

Garuda Indonesia, formerly Garuda Indonesian Airways, the national carrier of Indonesia, was founded on March 31 1950, by the government and KLM. Its aim was to replace the post-war Inter-Island Division of KLM and the pre-war KNILM. In 1954 nationalization took place. On January 1 1963, Garuda took over De Kkroonduif's domestic operations in West New Guinea. A year later however, they were handed over to PT Merpati Nusantara, the nationalized domestic operator. In October 1978 Garuda took over the company. Today the airline operates scheduled passenger and cargo services from its base in Jakarta to London (LGW), Amsterdam, Frankfurt, Paris (CDG), Rome, Zurich, Athens, Abu Dhabi, Jeddah, Bangkok, Kuala Lumpur, Penang, Singapore, Hong Kong, Manila, Sydney, Perth, Melbourne, Honolulu, and to Tokyo (NRT) via Denpasar. Garuda's domestic network extends one-tenth of the way round the world, linking Jakarta with over thirty points throughout the archipelago. The company has various subsidiaries, including hotels, catering firms and travel agents. In September 1985 a brand new livery was introduced, when a DC-10 was repainted to coincide with the Indonesian President's European visit. The dramatic new image, designed by Walter Landor and Associates of San Francisco, centres on a bird motif. This consists of five stripes, which represent the five national ideals. These appear in various shades of light blue and turquoise, which get progressively greener from nose to tail. It is displayed on the all-dark blue fin alongside new style 'Garuda Indonesia' titles, also in dark blue. A white fuselage contrasts smartly with the blue tail and titles. The national flag appears alongside the forward passenger door. Today the fleet consists of Fokker F-28, Airbus A300, Douglas DC-9, DC-10 and Boeing 747 aircraft. As part of a fleet renewal programme, Garuda has ordered the Fokker 100 and Boeing 737-300 to replace the F-28 and DC-9. A Boeing 747-200, PK-GSC, is seen here whilst taxiing at Jakarta, after arriving on flight GA883 from London Gatwick, via Brussels and Abu Dhabi. The carrier's ICAO call sign is 'INDONESIA'. *(Garuda Indonesia)*

GULF AIR (GF/GFA) Oman

Gulf Air was originally formed in March 1950 as Gulf Aviation Co. Ltd., by N. Bosworth and a number of Bahraini shareholders. Scheduled passenger services began on July 5 of that year, using Avro Anson equipment. The present name was adopted in early 1973, and since April 1 1974, the company shares have been held by the governments of the Gulf States of Bahrain, Oman, Qatar, and the United Arab Emirates. It should be noted however, that of the seven UAE states, only Abu Dhabi has a financial stake in the airline, and only Sharjah recognises Gulf Air as its official carrier. It is even more interesting to point out that the majority of the airline's fleet is Omani (A40) registered. In 1985 the carrier ceased services to Dubai, which set up its own official carrier, Emirates Airlines. Today Gulf Air operates a network of scheduled passenger and cargo operations linking Bahrain with Abu Dhabi, Al Fujeirah, Amman, Athens, Bangkok, Bombay, Cairo, Colombo, Dacca, Damascus, Dar-es-Salaam, Dhahran, Delhi, Doha, Frankfurt, Hong Kong, Istanbul, Jeddah, Karachi, Khartoum, Kuwait, Larnaca, London (LHR), Muscat, Manila, Nairobi, New York (JFK) (in conjunction with TWA), Paris (ORY), Ras Al Khaimah, Riyadh, Salalah, Sana'a, and Sharjah. Charter work is also undertaken. Subsidiary companies include Bahrain Airport Services, Gulf Helicopters, Gulf Hotels, Abu Dhabi Airport Services and Doha Airport Services. A fleet of Boeing 737-200, 767-300ER, and L-1011 Tristar aircraft is maintained. A Boeing 747-200, LN-AET, was leased from SAS, but was returned in 1987. The aircraft depicted here, N203AE, is however, no longer with the company; having been leased from Middle East Airlines on leasing contract from 1985 to 1986. It can be seen at London's Heathrow Airport, awaiting routine maintenance by British Airways. Gulf Air's striking livery employs an all-white fuselage which displays an extended 'chin flash' in the national colours of the individual states, purple, green and red. The top half of the fin is similarly coloured, below which appears a detailed 'Golden Falcon' motif, alongside suitable gold lettering. Fuselage titling, in bold green letters reads 'Gulf Air' in English and Arabic, with the former being given precedence on both sides. The company's ICAO call sign is 'GULF'. *(K.G. Wright)*

HIGHLAND EXPRESS
AIRWAYS (VY)

United Kingdom

Highland Express, Scotland's national airline, was originally formed in July 1984 by Sir Ranulph Fiennes and a group of businessmen which, at that time included Richard Branson. Following a series of non-starts, through lack of finances, aircraft and other requirements, the CAA finally gave its authority for the company to fly between London (STN), Birmingham and Glasgow (PIK) to New York (EWR) and Toronto. Due to a breakdown in negotiations between Britain and Canada at that time, the latter service was never operated. A single Boeing 747-123, G-HIHO, previously with American Airlines as N14939, was utilized over the less than lucrative routes. For five days a week it flew the Atlantic; Stansted and Birmingham being served on alternate days. The latter route was soon dropped, due to a lack of passengers. With loads dropping even further, a once-weekly London to Brussels service was opened. This was to coincide with the aircraft's maintenance checks with Sabena. Then Highland Express took to flying passengers, be it at a special fare, between Stansted and Prestwick. This was basically one of a number of last ditch efforts to fill its 450-seat aircraft. However, this was to no avail, and in December 1987, less than five months after

the inaugural flight, Highland Express ceased operations. During the last few weeks of operation, the airline had gone to the effort of basing its 747 at Prestwick, and then leasing a BAe 1-11 to operate the connecting service to Stansted. At the time of cessation Sabena had impounded the aircraft at Brussels, due to non-payment of maintenance fees. Citycorp, the leasing company who owned the 747, was itself owed many millions of dollars. Attempts to re-start the airline were made, but to no avail. The Highland Express livery was extremely bold for such a large aircraft. With the Boeing 747 resplendent in a very smart blue and white scheme, the colours had been taken from the Scottish national flag of St. Andrew, which was flown on the tail. A broad matching windowline underlined similarly coloured 'Highland Express' roof titles and registration on the rear cabin section, which was preceded by the British Union flag. The engine nacelles were also painted white. As a footnote, G-HIHO was returned to Citycorp who leased it to Qantas, as VH-EEI. The aircraft is currently in service with Air Pacific (see separate entries).
(Flying Colours)

IBERIA (IB/IBE)
Spain

In 1921, the Compania Espanola de Trafico Aereo was formed with a fleet of two converted DC-4 light bomber biplanes. Mail services were operated daily between Seville and Larache in Morocco. In 1925, the first Spanish passenger airline was founded. Union Aerea Espanola was formed to operate domestic and external routes using four passenger Junkers F13s. Iberia was established on June 25 1927, and permission was granted to operate air services between Madrid and Barcelona. In 1928, the three Spanish airlines were merged into one company, CLASSA, and on December 31 of that year, it entered into contract with the Government to provide air services. It subsequently expanded, and on May 27 1929, new services were inaugurated between Madrid and Seville. During 1931 the airline was reformed as LAPE (Lineas Aereas Postales Espanoles); with subsequent permission being granted for a Bordeaux-Paris route. A service between Madrid, Casablanca and Las Palmas was added the same year. Iberia replaced LAPE as the official name in 1937, and in 1940 was designated the 'flag' carrier of Spain. Following the war, Iberia embarked upon re-building its international network. The first Madrid-London (Croydon) service in May 1946 was followed by a Madrid-Paris line, later that year. Caracas, San Juan, Mexico City and Havana were added between 1949 and 1950. In 1970 the Boeing 747 entered service with Iberia, replacing the DC-8 on key transatlantic routes. In 1982 it became a member of the 'Atlas Group', joining Air France, Alitalia, Sabena and Lufthansa in Europe's premier technical cooperative venture. Today Iberia serves eighty-one destinations in forty-six countries. A fleet of Douglas DC-9, DC-10, Boeing 727, 737, 747, and Airbus A300 aircraft is maintained. Orders for the A320 and MD87 are outstanding. A regal livery combines the colours of the flag with an easy clue to the country's holiday attraction. Triple cheatlines in red, orange and yellow start on the cabin roof, behind the cockpit and sweep along the length of the white fuselage as a windowline. An 'IB' tail motif in red and yellow includes a small gold crown representing Spain's return to democratic monarchy. The Iberia tail logo is carried in white on the fuselage and occasionally in red on the engines. The carrier's ICAO call sign is 'IBERIA'. (K.G. Wright)

ICELANDAIR (FI/ICE)   Iceland

Icelandair was founded on June 3 1937 under the name of Flugfelag Akureyar and commenced scheduled passenger services using a single Waco floatplane, between Akureyri and Reykjavik. Subsequent changes of name occurred in 1940, when the title Flugfelag Islands was adopted, followed by the present title in 1956. In July 1973 the company was merged with Icelandic Airways, and was set up in its present form the following month. Today Icelandair is one hundred per cent privately owned, with over 3,500 shareholders. It is famous for its low cost international services, and in recent years has been Europe's fastest growing carrier. Scheduled passenger and cargo services link Reykjavik with New York (JFK), Chicago, Boston (BWI), Detroit, Orlando, Paris (ORY), London (LHR), Glasgow, Oslo, Stockholm, Gothenburg, Bergen, Copenhagen, Frankfurt, Salzburg, Luxembourg, the Faroe Islands, and Kulusuk and Narssarssuaq in Greenland. The carrier also operates an eleven-point domestic scheduled network, together with international and domestic charter flights. Subsidiary and associate companies include Eagle Air (Arnarflug), North Air, East Air (domestic airlines), Cargolux and

Urval Travel Bureau. A fleet of Boeing 727, Douglas DC-8 and Fokker F-27 aircraft is maintained. On order for delivery commencing April 1989 are two Boeing 737-400 types; which will replace the smaller, less economical, Boeing 727s already operated. During 1982, Icelandair leased a Boeing 747-143, as depicted here at Copenhagen Airport. The aircraft was registered N356AS, having previously served with Alitalia as I-DEME. It is however, no longer with the fleet, having been returned at the end of that year. The airline's colourscheme consists of a conventionally shaped windowline in medium black, and is trimmed by a similarly coloured parallel pinstripe. Simple black 'Icelandair' lettering is reproduced on the upper forward fuselage, a short distance from the Icelandic flag. It should be noted that domestic aircraft sport the alternate 'Flugleidir' titles, the Icelandic equivalent, but on an otherwise identical scheme. The company motif, worn on the tail, represents the initial 'F' of Flugleidir on the port side, but on the opposite side is the mirrored image. The carrier's ICAO call sign is 'ICEAIR'.
(K.G. Wright)

IRAN AIR (IR/IRA)

Iran

Iran Air was formed in February 1962 as the successor to the private carriers, Iranian Airways and Persian Air Services, which were merged into a national airline, wholly owned by the Government. Today Iran Air (the Airline of The Islamic Republic of Iran), also known as Homa, an acronym of its Persian name, has suffered badly as a result of the Gulf War. Since the rise to power of the Ayatollah Khomeini in 1979, the airline's operations have been dramatically curtailed. Prior to the demise of the Shah, Iran Air had been operating to twenty-nine destinations, ranging as far west as New York (JFK), and as far east as Tokyo (NRT); at that stage there were over one hundred weekly departures. It had also been hoped that the airline would purchase the Concorde, and were the final carrier to cancel their order for the supersonic aircraft. Today scheduled passenger and cargo services are operated to thirteen domestic points, Abadan, Bandar Abbas, Bushehr, Chah-Bahar, Isfahan, Kerman, Kish Island, Mashad, Rasht, Shiraz, Tabriz, Yazd and Zahedan. International cities served are Abu Dhabi, Athens, Beijing, Bombay, Damascus, Doha, Dubai, Frankfurt, Geneva, Istanbul, Karachi, Larnaca, London (LHR), Paris (ORY), Rome, Sharjah, Tokyo (NRT), and Vienna. Charter flights are also undertaken. A fleet of Boeing 707-300, 727-100, 737-200, 747-200, 747SP-86, Fokker F-27, and Airbus A300B2 aircraft is maintained. Following the overthrow of the Shah, a small addition was made to the traditional livery. This was in the form of the large black 'Iran Air' fuselage titles being reduced in size, to allow for small 'The Airline of The Islamic Republic of Iran' subtitles and a representation of the new Iranian flag. The conventional blue cheatline arrangement and tail colouring remained unchanged, as did the mythical 'Homma Bird' which has always dominated the fin. It should be noted that the company name also appears on the rear fuselage in Farshi script. Pure-freight aircraft can be identified by the additional 'Cargo' titles next to the 'Iran Air' lettering. EP-ICC, a Boeing 747-2J9F, can be seen here whilst on approach to London Heathrow Airport's runway 27R. The carrier's ICAO call sign is 'IRANAIR'. *(K.G. Wright)*

JAPAN AIR LINES (JL/JAL)

Japan

Japan Air Lines is the successor to the original privately-owned company of the same name, which began operating in August 1951. The new JAL came into being in October 1953 as the national airline with a Government holding of fifty per cent. Today the carrier is fully privately owned. With 52,893 shareholders, the Japanese Government sold its 34.5 per cent stake in 1987. In 1986 JAL lost its monopoly of scheduled international passenger services, when All Nippon Airways began operations to Guam, Los Angeles and Washington. However, the airline was able to launch its first new domestic services since 1972, linking Tokyo (HND) with Kagoshima and Komatsu, and Nagoya with Fukuoka. In April 1986 JAL launched nonstop Tokyo (NRT)-London (LHR) and Tokyo (NRT)-Paris (CDG) flights. The airline is the world's largest Boeing 747 operator, with one of the type currently in use, the 300SR, seating an awesome 563 passengers. Today, JAL operates an extensive network of scheduled passenger and cargo services, covering fifty-nine cities in thirty-four countries. Services link Tokyo (NRT), Osaka, Naha, Sapporo, Fukuoka, Kagoshima and Nagoya with numerous points in Asia and the Middle East, Australia (Sydney), New Zealand (Auckland),

North America (Anchorage, Vancouver, Seattle, Atlanta, Honolulu, San Francisco, Los Angeles, Chicago and New York (JFK)), Central America (Mexico City), South America (Rio de Janeiro), and Europe (London (LHR), Paris (CDG), Amsterdam, Dusseldorf, Copenhagen, Hamburg, Frankfurt, Zurich, Rome, Athens and Madrid), and Moscow. A fleet of Boeing 747, 767 and DC-10 aircraft is maintained. Delivery of the 747-400 is awaited. The colourscheme consists of only two colours, with the red of the national flag contrasting with the black, to give a 'clean cut' image. The tail emblem, also known as a 'Tsuru', consists of a large rising sun formed by the outstretched wings of a red crane, with white 'JAL' lettering. Above dual red and black windowlines appear 'Japan Air Lines' titles in black, alongside the Japanese flag, and the whole colourscheme is enhanced by the highly polished, natural metal undersides. Freighter aircraft can be recognised by the 'JAL Cargo' lettering, in thicker script, on the forward fuselage instead of the normal titling. JA8151, a Boeing 747-246F SCD, is seen here on departure from Heathrow Airport. The ICAO call sign is 'JAPANAIR'. *(B.T. Richards)*

JAPAN ASIA AIRWAYS (EG/JAA)

Japan

Japan Asia Airways, a wholly-owned subsidiary of Japan Air Lines, was formed on August 8 1975, to take over the Tokyo (NRT)-Taipei (CKS) route. This had been vacated a year earlier by the parent company. Today, Japan Asia operates scheduled passenger and cargo services, as well as charters, from Tokyo (NRT and HDA), Osaka and Okinawa to Taipei (CKS), Kaohsiung, Taichung, Hong Kong, Guam, and Saipan. A fleet of Douglas DC-10 and Boeing 747 aircraft is operated. JAA operates three types of service on its Boeing aircraft. First, Rainbow (Club), and Economy Class allow a wide range of fares to be offered. The DC-10 types however, do not have a First Class, due to space restrictions, and the fact that they are utilised on the company's lesser routes. All of the aircraft used by Japan Asia wear a livery which is based on that of the Japanese flag carrier. This includes the national airline's narrow red and black cheatlines, but with the black 'Japan Air Lines' roof titling replaced by similarly-coloured, but newly-designed 'Japan Asia' lettering. The 'red crane' JAL tail motif has been dropped in favour of a brand new symbol which features a red 'rising sun', and a superimposed, oriental-styled, initial 'A'. Most of the company's fleet is owned by the airline, with the occasional aircraft being leased-in from Japan Air Lines as necessary. The airline has been utilizing Boeing 747-100 types, so it came as a big increase in capacity when Japan Asia took delivery of its first 747-300, in October 1988. The carrier's ICAO call sign is 'ASIA'. A Boeing 747-146 can be seen here at Tokyo. *(Flying Colours)*

KLM — ROYAL DUTCH AIRLINES (KL/KLM)

The Netherlands

KLM has the distinction of being the world's oldest airline. It is able to trace its roots as far back as October 7 1919. Operations commenced when services were initiated between Amsterdam and London in 1920; a two-passenger de Havilland D.H. 16 being used. Other European cities were later added, and in 1929 services were extended to Java. Operations were begun in the East Indies during 1935, and these were continued throughout the Second World War, thus enabling KLM to claim over sixty-eight years of nonstop operations. Wholly-owned subsidiaries include KLM Aerocarto, KLM Helicopters, NLM City Hopper and Netherlines. Holdings are also held in Air UK, Transavia, Martinair, Schreiner Aviation and XP Express Parcel Systems. The national flag carrier of The Netherlands operates a network of scheduled passenger and cargo services from Amsterdam to 129 cities in seventy-nine countries, spread throughout Europe; North, Central and South America, Africa, the Near, Middle and Far East, as well as to Australia. KLM operates a fleet of Boeing 737, 747, DC-9, DC-10, A310 and Fokker F100 aircraft. Outstanding orders for the Boeing 737-400 and Boeing 747-400 are awaited. The two tones of blue that appear in today's livery have been used for over thirty years in various forms. A deep blue windowline is flanked by a bold white stripe below, and an all-light blue cabin roof above, displaying a reversed out white registration and fuselage logo. The latter appears in a comparatively small form. The fin is all white and promotes the company logo which consists of dark blue 'KLM' letters, topped by a light blue stylised crown, to emphasise the 'Royal' Dutch Airlines. PH-BUW, a Boeing 747-306 SCD, is seen here at Amsterdam's Schipol Airport. The aircraft, a Combi, was delivered in September 1986; and is named Leonardo da Vinci. The carrier's ICAO call sign is 'KLM'. *(K.G. Wright)*

KOREAN AIR (KE/KAL)   South Korea

Korean Air, known until 1984 as Korean Air Lines, is one of the world's fastest growing carriers. The company was formed in June 1962 when it succeeded Korean National Airlines (founded in 1948). KAL was originally wholly owned by the Government of Korea, but was acquired by the Han Jin Group in 1969. The carrier operates scheduled passenger and cargo services from Seoul, Pusan and Cheju to Tokyo (NRT), Osaka, Fukuoka, Nagoya, Niigata, Taipei (CKS), Hong Kong, Bangkok, Singapore, Manila, Kuala Lumpur, Dhahran, Baghdad, Abu Dhabi, Tripoli, London (LGW), Zurich, Frankfurt, Amsterdam, Paris (CDG), Los Angeles, Honolulu and New York (JFK). Korean Air plans to launch additional services to Toronto, Vancouver, Rome and Sydney. A fleet of Boeing 707, 727, 747, DC-10, MD82, A300, DHC-8, Dauphin, F-27 and F-28 aircraft is utilized. Delivery of new generation 747-400 and MD11 area aircraft is also awaited; KAL was a launch customer for the latter type in December 1986. Korean Air's impressive new image was unveiled in early 1984, when it replaced the previous red, white and blue 'Korean Air Lines" scheme which dated back to the sixties. In what was perhaps an unusual step, the carrier decided not only to change the livery design, but also to adopt a brand new company motif, and more dynamic title all in one move. A pale shade of blue covers the entire upper fuselage half, representing the sky, whilst below runs a silver cheatline, with the undersides in a pale grey. The company logo, known as the 'Taeguk', combines the red and blue of heaven and earth. White has been added to represent the 'never ending strength of progress'. This appears on the tail fin and forms the letter 'O' within the blue 'Korean Air' fuselage titles. HL7456, a Boeing 747SP-B5, can be seen here at New York's JFK International Airport, having recently arrived from Seoul. The aircraft was operating the nonstop flight KE026. The carrier's ICAO call sign is 'KOREANAIR'. *(K.G. Wright)*

KUWAIT AIRWAYS CORPORATION (KU/KAC)

Kuwait

Kuwait Airways, the country's national flag carrier, was formed in March 1954 by a group of local businessmen, under the name Kuwait National Airways Company. Its aim was to operate a fleet of Douglas DC-3s between Kuwait and Beirut. The airline was renamed the Kuwait Airways Company three years later. British Overseas Airways Corporation took over technical management under a five-year contract in May 1958, and British International Airlines was completely absorbed in April 1959. The carrier became wholly Government-owned in June 1962. In April 1964 KAC absorbed Trans Arabia Airways. Today the carrier provides scheduled passenger and cargo services from Kuwait to forty-one cities in thirty-eight countries in the Middle and Far East, Europe, North Africa and North America. Subsidiaries include Kuwait

Aviation Services Company — KASCO, a catering firm. A fleet of Boeing 727, 747, 767, A300 and A310 aircraft is maintained. BAe 125-700s and Gulfstream 3s are used on purely VIP and executive flights. An attractive shade of ocean blue was chosen as the colour to adorn the windowline and tail band, trimmed either side in black in both cases. The latter contains the company's stylised bird logo. English and Arabic titling reads 'Kuwait Airways' in blue, giving precedence to the latter language on the starboard side and the former on the port. Tail lettering in separate languages appears on either side. The national flag appears at the top of the tail. 9K-ADC, a Boeing 747-269B SCD, is seen here at Geneva. The aircraft was operating flight KU1143 from Kuwait. Kuwait Airways' ICAO call sign is 'KUWAITI'. *(K.G. Wright)*

LIONAIR (GZ/LIR)
Luxembourg

Lionair was formed at the end of 1987 through a joint project with Luxair, the Luxembourg national carrier, and Cargolux, the all-freight airline. Its aim is to perform passenger services on behalf of other carriers and tour operators. The share capital is divided up, so that Luxair holds fifty-five per cent, whilst Cargolux owns forty-five per cent. The headquarters of this new company are located at Luxembourg's Findel Airport. Lionair commenced operations in February 1988 using two wide-bodied Boeing 747-100 aircraft, each of which have a seating capacity of 505 passengers. Services are flown worldwide. An example of these are those that are operated by the tour operator, Airtours, between May and December 1988. From London (STN), via Manchester, flights were made to Kingston (Jamaica), and Santo Domingo (Dominican Republic). Direct services were flown from Manchester to Barbados. Cargolux has acquired an excellent knowledge of the leasing of wide-bodied aircraft, whilst Luxair has great experience in passenger transportation and inclusive tour services. The two partners have a belief that they can fill a real market gap in this field of the airline industry.

During March 1988 Boeing 747-121, LX-FCV, was rolled out at Paris (ORY) wearing the full red and white livery of Lionair. A stylised red Lion's head is displayed on the fin above black company titles. A narrow red cheatline arrangement, positioned below window level, has been used to divide the white (upper) and natural metal (lower) fuselage colouring. No titling adorns the forward fuselage since this is left for the specific airline, or tour company, leasing the aircraft. LX-GCV, the airline's second 747-121, is seen here at London's Stansted Airport in June 1988, whilst operating a flight on behalf of Orion Air (ICAO call sign 'TAG'). Both of Lionair's aircraft were originally with Pan Am as N754PA and N770PA respectively, having been built in 1970. It should be noted that in July 1988, the carrier leased a Boeing 747-283B, LX-OCV, from Guinness Peat Aviation; this aircraft immediately being sub-leased to Garuda for two months, before being returned to the Irish leasing firm. The carrier's ICAO call sign is 'LIONAIR'; although it is used only for positioning flights, since the relevant two/three-letter code, and call sign, are provided by the leasing company at that particular time. *(K.G. Wright)*

LUFTHANSA GERMAN AIRLINES (LH/DLH)

Federal Republic of Germany

Lufthansa was originally founded in January 1926 as Deutsche Luft Hansa, following a merger of Aero Lloyd and Junkers Luftverkehr. The flying crane motif however, originated with Deutsche Luft-rederei in 1919. The company was reformed as Luftag on January 6 1953, and adopted the present title in August of the following year. Operations however, did not commence until April 1955. Today Lufthansa operates an extensive worldwide system of scheduled passenger and cargo services to 149 points in seventy-eight countries in Europe, Africa, the Near, Middle, and Far East, Australia, and North, Central and South America. The company operates various subsidiaries, these include Condor Flugdienst, German Cargo Services, Lufthansa Services GmbH, Lufthansa Commercial Holding GmbH, AFS-Aviation Fuel Services GmbH, and Delvag Luftfahrtversicherungs AG. Lufthansa also has a forty per cent holding in DLT. It was one of the launch customers for the wide-bodied all new Airbus A340. In 1987 it undertook an internal reorganisation to cut overheads and streamline operations and

sales. The Federal German Government currently holds seventy-four per cent of Lufthansa's shares, while the remainder is held by the State of North Rhine Westphalia, Federal German Railways and private investors. The carrier operates a fleet of Boeing 727, 737, 747, DC-10, A300, A300 and A320 aircraft. Outstanding orders are pending for the A330, A340 and Boeing 747-400. Although during the past fifteen years a number of experimental variations have been tried, Lufthansa continues to stay with its traditional dark blue and yellow livery. The dark blue 'flying crane' logo is displayed on the all-blue tail within a yellow disk, and is repeated under the cockpit windows, as well as on each engine in blue outline. The cheatline, also in dark blue, runs at window level, surmounted by similarly coloured 'Lufthansa' titles. Most types in the fleet sport natural metal undersides, apart from the Airbus types which have grey undersides. Boeing 747-230B SCD, D-ABZE, is seen here at Frankfurt, on push back. The aircraft was departing on flight LH746 to Hong Kong. The carrier's ICAO call sign is 'LUFTHANSA'. (K.G. Wright)

LUXAIR (LG/LGL)   Luxembourg

Luxair, the national carrier of the Grand Duchy of Luxembourg, was formed in 1961 as Luxembourg Airlines, after it had become plainly obvious to the Government that the maintenance regular airlinks with its neighbouring countries were absolutely essential. On April 2 1962, utilizing a single Fokker F-27, leased from the manufacturer, scheduled passenger services to Paris (CDG), Frankfurt and Amsterdam were initiated; technical assistance was being provided by KLM. Today, Luxair's scheduled route network links Luxembourg with a number of major European cities including Amsterdam, Frankfurt, London (LHR), Athens, Zurich, Paris (CDG), Palma and Rome. Regular holiday flights, flown on behalf of Luxair Tours, a travel company subsidiary, are operated to Bastia, Corfu, Catania, Agadir, Ibiza, Malaga, Nice, Rhodes, Rimini, Dubrovnik, the Canary Islands, and Johannesburg (South Africa). In addition to the Luxembourg Government, with 20.91 per cent stake, other shareholders in Luxair include Luxembourg Steel Industries (12.14 per cent), International Bank of Luxembourg (12.14 per cent), General Bank of Luxembourg (12.14 per cent), Compagnie Luxembourgoise de Telediffusion (12.14 per cent), Luxair Finance (18.18 per cent) and private interests (0.21 per cent). A fleet of Boeing 737, 747SP, F-27 and Metro III aircraft is maintained. The latter type is operated by the company's subsidiary, Luxair Commuter. Delivery of the Fokker 50 is pending, to eventually replace its older sister, the F-27. Luxair's colourscheme makes use of just the blue and white elements of the national flag. The distinctive shade of blue colours both the broad windowline and the tail background colour, thus promoting the company's white motif which usually points forward; although on some aircraft it is reversed. 'Luxair' titling appears on an all-white cabin roof. The F-27s wear a variation to the livery, in that their tails are white, with a blue company motif. Boeing 747SP-44, LX-LGX, can be seen here having operated flight LG182 from Jan Smuts' Airport, Johannesburg. The aircraft is leased from South African Airways, and operates in an all economy 307-seat layout. It should be noted that the Boeing aircraft is sub-leased to Luxavia, another of Luxair's subsidiary holiday company's. The carrier's ICAO call sign is 'LUXAIR'. *(U. Schaefer Collection)*

MALAYSIA AIRLINES (MH/MAS)

Malaysia

Malaysia Airlines was formed in April 1971 after the cessation of the Malaysia-Singapore Airlines consortium. Originally known as Malaysian Airline System, initial services commenced on October 1 1972 over a domestic network. Initially the company was a wholly-owned Government entity but, following a privatisation exercise at the end of 1985, the Malaysian Government's equity participation was reduced to seventy per cent. This was then further diminished, and by March 31 1987, the Government's shareholding stood at fifty-two per cent — this comprising forty-two per cent held by the Ministry of Finance (Incorporated) and five per cent each for the Sarawak and Sabah State Governments. Following a dramatic increase in international coverage and to create greater awareness of the airline and country in the marketplace, a new name and corporate image was introduced. The freshly renamed Malaysia Airlines took to the skies on October 15 1987; with it going a restyled kite to project movement and dynamism. The company today operates an extensive network of scheduled domestic flights to over thirty-four points plus international services to Singapore, Jakarta, Hatyai, Bandar Seri Begawan, Medan, Manila, Hong Kong, Taipei (CKS), Tokyo (NRT), Dubai, Amman, Colombo, Denpasar, Bangkok, Melbourne, Perth, Sydney, Madras, Seoul, Honolulu, Los Angeles, Amsterdam, Jeddah, London (LHR), Frankfurt, and Paris (CDG). The airline has equity participation in three major associate companies, the Pan Pacific Hotel in Kuala Lumpur, Malaysia Helicopter Services, and Pelangi Air Sdn Bhd, Malaysia's domestic airline, which commenced operations in 1988. A fleet of Douglas DC-10, Airbus A300, Fokker F-27, DHC-6 Twin Otters, Boeing 737 and 747 aircraft is maintained. A fleet of Fokker 50 types are being delivered between August 1989 and March 1990, to replace the F-27s. Gearing itself up for greater expansion, new destinations being sort after include Delhi, Karachi, Istanbul, Zurich, Copenhagen, and a second port in Japan. Malaysia Airlines' new livery is striking and colourful. An all-white fin displays a bold representation of the traditional Kalantan Kite motif, in red and blue. This overlooks the fuselage top, also in white, and blue lower case 'Malaysia' titles. The national flag precedes the company name on the port side, and follows it on the starboard. The carrier's ICAO call sign is 'MALAYSIAN'. *(Malaysian Airlines)*

MARTINAIR HOLLAND (MP/MPH)

The Netherlands

Martinair Holland was formed in May 1958 as Martin's Air Charter; its purpose being to operate aerial advertising and joy rides, using a Douglas DC-3. The present title was adopted in 1974. In the Spring of 1988, the company commenced scheduled transatlantic passenger services from Amsterdam to Baltimore, Boston, Chicago, Cleveland, Detroit, Los Angeles, Miami, Minneapolis, New York (JFK), San Francisco, Seattle and Toronto. The major part of the company's business, however, is the operation of worldwide passenger and cargo charters. In addition, the carrier provides complete inclusive tour packages and operates air taxi and executive flights. Martinair maintains and operates the Dutch Government's Fokker F-28, which is used by members of the Royal Family and cabinet ministers. Shareholders are the Royal Nedlloyd Group (49.2 per cent), KLM (29.8 per cent) and various financial institutions (twenty-one per cent). Associate companies are active in the fields of flight training, sales support by hostess teams, party catering and the production of deep freeze meals and components. In Amsterdam the MartINN restaurant is operated. Martinair operates a fleet of Boeing 747, 767, DC-10, A310, MD82, Citation II and Cessna 404 Titan aircraft. The carrier's colourscheme displays a deep red windowline, which on the MD82s, Citations and Titan, doubles back to form a stylised red 'M' tail logo. However, on the A310, DC-10, Boeing 747 and 767, the tail logo and cheatlines are distinctly separate. Black 'Martinair Holland' fuselage titles bodly announce the company name. This is repeated on the third engine of the DC-10s. The lower fuselage is painted grey on the A310s, but left in natural metal on the other aircraft. PH-MCE, a Boeing 747-21AC Combi SCD, can be seen here on its take-off roll from Amsterdam's Schipol Airport. The aircraft is operating flight MP607 to Miami. The ICAO call sign for the company is 'MARTINAIR'.
(K.G. Wright)

MIDDLE EAST AIRLINES (ME/MEA)

Lebanon

Middle East Airlines was formed in May 1945 by a group of Lebanese businessmen. The company's first service was from Beirut to Nicosia on November 20 of that year, utilizing a de Havilland Dragon Rapide aircraft. The route was subsequently extended to the Iraqi capital, Baghdad. From those early beginnings, the airline greatly expanded its services. This was aided when a merger took place in November 1965 with Air Liban, and the acquisition four years later of the traffic rights of Lebanese International Airlines. Middle East Airlines is currently owned by Inta Investments (62.5 per cent), and Air France (28.5 per cent). The carrier has been through a period of troubled times with the Lebanese war. Aircraft of the national airline have literally been blown apart whilst on the tarmac at Beirut airport, so it was subsequently decided to move its operations to Paris (ORY). Currently, MEA serves Abidjan, Abu Dhabi, Aden, Amman, Ankara, Athens, Bahrain, Brussels, Cairo, Copenhagen, Damascus, Dhahran, Doha, Dubai, Frankfurt, Freetown, Geneva, Istanbul, Jeddah, Kano, Khartoum, Kuwait, Lagos, Larnaca, London (LHR), Madrid, Milan, Monrovia, Muscat, Nice, Paris (ORY), Rome, Tunis and Zurich. A fleet of Boeing 707 and 720 aircraft is operated. Due to the current situation in the Lebanon, the airline is unable to re-equip due to insecurity and the extremely high insurance costs. Three Boeing 747s are owned, however these are leased out to various carriers, including British Airways. In December 1987, MEA introduced a new livery. This design features a revised cheatline arrangement which incorporates the legend 'NEW Q' on the forward fuselage. The red tail colouring, which now commences further up the tail in a similar style to the cheatlines, accommodates the traditional cedar tree motif as before. 'MEA' titles occupy their usual positions on the cabin roof, whilst the fuselage undersides and engines have now been painted pale grey. EI-BPH, a Boeing 747-133, was leased between June and September 1985 from Guinness Peat Aviation, and was to serve on Paris (ORY) to New York (JFK) route that the company had. The carrier's ICAO call sign is 'CEDAR JET'.
(K.G. Wright)

MINERVE (FQ/MIN)   France

In June 1975, Rene F. Meyer founded Minerve, the French supplemental airline. It was not however, until November of that year that the company commenced passenger and cargo charter operations to various points in Europe, the Middle East, Africa, the Far East and the Americas. At that time Minerve's fleet comprised SE-210 Caravelle and Douglas DC-8 equipment. In August 1986 the airline initiated charter flights from Paris (ORY) to Point-a-Pitre, Papeete and Fort de France. Thus, Minerve successfully broke a long-standing monopoly that UTA had on the Papeete route. The company has operational bases at Paris (Orly) and Nimes-Garons. In addition, Minerve also undertakes maintenance work for other carriers. European destinations are still serviced by two Caravelle aircraft, as well as two MD-83 types. The latter examples being leased-in from the Irish leasing firm, Irish Aerospace. Prior to the delivery of the first MD83 in March 1987, Minerve's colourscheme was plain and uninspiring. With its red windowline, matching roof titles and plain white tail, it was decided that it would be unsuitable for application to the new flagship. Therefore a new corporate

image was designed. This featured the head of the Roman goddess Minerva, after whom the airline is named, within a red circle on the fin. Below the windowline, fuselage stripes in burgundy, white, blue and red, are broken to accommodate red 'Minerve' titling. The national flag is situated to the rear, above the windowline. December 8 of that year saw the delivery of the airline's first wide-bodied aircraft, a Boeing 747-283B. Registered F-GHBM, it is on a lease agreement from GPA Aviation. Previously, the aircraft was registered LN-AET, and had seen service with such companies as Nigerian Airways and SAS (see separate entries). It can be seen here, during April 1988, being towed towards its departure gate at Paris (Orly). Minerve's current route network includes Asuncion (Paraguay), Banjul (Gambia), Bridgetown (Barbados), Dakar (Senegal), Havana (Cuba), Honolulu (USA), Kathmandu (Nepal), Kingston (Jamaica), Lima (Peru), Managua (Nicaragua), Mombasa (Kenya), Nassau (Bahamas), Panama City (Panama), and Rangoon (Burma). The carrier's ICAO call sign is 'MINERVE'. *(K.G. Wright)*

NIGERIA AIRWAYS (WT/NGA)

Nigeria

Nigeria Airways, the national flag carrier of the oil rich African country of Nigeria, was founded in 1958. Its aim was to take over the country's air services, formerly operated by West African Airways Corporation. Today the airline serves destinations in East and West Africa and operates high profile flights from Lagos, Kano, and Port Harcourt to London (LHR), Amsterdam, Paris (CDG), Rome, New York (JFK) and Jeddah. A large domestic network links major points in all nineteen states in the Nigerian Federation with key cities in the country. The airline is now wholly owned by the Nigerian Federal Government. A fleet of Douglas DC-10, Airbus A310, Boeing 707 and Boeing 737 aircraft is operated. The Boeing 747-200 Combi that Nigeria Airways were leasing, LN-AET, was repossessed by GPA Aviation and subsequently leased out to Minerve, the French supplemental carrier (see separate entry). The green and white colouring of the airline has been provided by the national flag, which itself appears on the tail fin, superimposed with the green 'flying elephant' company logo. Twin green cheatlines are separated by a narrow white windowline and highlight the bold green 'Nigeria Airways' fuselage lettering, which appears in upper case characters. The lower fuselage is left in a natural metal finish. This is in direct contrast with a white roof on all types, with the exception of the Airbus A310, which has a grey underside. Prior to its return to GPA Aviation, the airline's Boeing 747 can be seen here at New York's JFK International Airport, having operated that day's flight WT852 from Lagos, via Monrovia, Liberia. The company's ICAO call sign is 'NIGERIA'. *(K.G. Wright)*

NORTHWEST AIRLINES (NW/NWA)

United States of America

The airline was founded in August 1926 as Northwest Airways; its objective being to transport mail under a US Post Office contract on the Chicago-St. Paul route. A name change to Northwest Orient was made in 1934. In 1986 an order for up to one hundred Airbus A320-200s was placed, and on August 2 of that year, Northwest merged with Republic Airlines. This strengthened the airline's US route system with major traffic hubs at Detroit, Minneapolis/St. Paul, and Memphis. The company has a marketing agreement with several regional airlines who operate feeder services under the name 'Northwest Airlink'. The carrier's livery and NW flight code is adopted for those aircraft operating those services. Northwest maintains an extensive network of scheduled passenger and cargo services in the USA and Canada. Transpacific flights are operated to Hawaii, Tokyo (NRT), Osaka, Seoul, Okinawa, Taipei (CKS), Manila, Hong Kong, Shanghai, Guam, Singapore (cargo only), and Bangkok. Transatlantic flights to London (LGW), Glasgow (PIK), Frankfurt, Copenhagen and Oslo are maintained. The carrier also serves Cancun and Puerto Vallerta, Montego Bay, and the Cayman Islands. A fleet of Boeing 727, 747, 757, DC-9, DC-10, MD82, Convair 580 and A320 aircraft is maintained. Orders for the A330 and A340 are outstanding. In 1989, Northwest initiated the first commercial Boeing 747-400 flights. Two of the type operated as flights NW 17 and NW 18 between New York (JFK) and Tokyo (NRT). This route is the carrier's longest, spanning 10,854 kilometres (6,744 miles) during the fourteen-hour flight over the Great Circle route. The Northwest livery is simple but distinctive, employing a broad white cheatline, dissecting the otherwise natural metal fuselage, which contains a dark blue shortened windowline and bright red 'Northwest' titling. The company motif is a red pointer indicating a northwest direction superimposed on a small red globe, and is carried relatively inconspicuously alongside the titles, but not on the tail, which is bright red overall. Occasionally, the national flag heads the fin. The entire fleet is adorned in this scheme, however, the natural metal appearance is often enhanced by a high degree of polish. Pure freight 747s have 'Northwest Cargo' titles, and are left an overall natural metal, devoid of white and blue cheatlines. The ICAO call sign is 'NORTHWEST'. *(Northwest Airlines)*

PAKISTAN INTERNATIONAL AIRLINES (PK/PIA)

Pakistan

Pakistan International, the country's state-owned carrier, was founded in 1954 to link East Pakistan with West Pakistan, now Bangladesh; Lockheed Super Constellation aircraft being used. The carrier had assistance from the Government as it had itself just taken over Orient Airways (founded in 1951), and the two airlines were subsequently merged. Today PIA currently operates scheduled passenger and cargo services to over thirty-one domestic points from its base at Karachi, and international routes to Tokyo (NRT), Beijing, Manila, Bangkok, Singapore, Kuala Lumpur, Colombo, Tehran, Dhahran, Kuwait, Baghdad, Damascus, Cairo, Amman, Tripoli, Istanbul, Athens, Rome, Frankfurt, Paris (ORY), Amsterdam, Copenhagen, London (LHR), New York (JFK), Muscat, Dubai, Abu Dhabi, Doha, Bahrain, Jeddah, Nairobi, Bombay, Delhi, Dhaka, Kathmandu, Riyadh, Moscow and Sana'a. The Government is the principal shareholder (sixty-one per cent), whilst the remainder is held primarily by private institutions. The airline's livery is based on the green and white national flag. This is enhanced by the regal appearance of a gold windowline. 'Pakistan International' titles in green, alongside their Urdu equivalent in gold, decorate the upper forward fuselage. This is in contrast to the very simple white 'PIA' tail logo. The distinctive green lower fuselage reaches down to wing level, with a grey painted underside. It should be noted that the last two letters of the registration are carried in white on the nose of the Boeing 707s only. The carrier operates a fleet of Boeing 707, 737, 747, DHC-6, Fokker F-27 and A300 aircraft types. A Boeing 747-200B is seen here at Frankfurt, having operated flight PK721 from Islamabad, via Karachi and Istanbul. This specific flight later carried on to New York (JFK). PIA's ICAO call sign is 'PAKISTAN'.

(K.G. Wright)

PAN AMERICAN WORLD AIRWAYS (PA/PAA)

United States of America

Pan Am was originally formed in March 1927, to operate a United States Postal Service contract between Key West in Florida and Havana in Cuba. Considerable international route expansion took place in the post-war years, so that by the 1960s the carrier had an extensive worldwide network of services. During 1979 the Metropolitan Air Facilities division (general aviation services), the Aerospace Services division (support for Kennedy Space Centre missile activities), and the Airline Services division (airline and airport technical and management assistance) were merged into Pan Am World Services, with headquarters at the striking Pan Am Building in New York City. The airline then became the second largest carrier in the USA in 1979, by acquiring a majority stockholding in National Airlines of Miami. Full integration of the two companies was implemented following the 1980 summer season. In February 1986 Pan Am sold its entire Pacific division to United Airlines, and on April 17 of that year, it acquired Ransome Airlines. This airline subsequently began services in the following June as 'Pan Am Express', feeding mainly into Pan Am's New York (JFK) hub. Today an extensive network of scheduled passenger services exists, covering over fifty-six destinations in the USA, fourteen in the Caribbean, ten in South America, plus Europe, the Middle East and Asia. The carrier is the largest operator at New York (JFK). Following the loss of its Pacific division, Pan Am concentrated on expanding its transatlantic services. Nine new European destinations (Leningrad, Moscow, Milan, Helsinki, Oslo, Stockholm, Prague, Krakow, and Shannon) were added in 1986. A network of local services in Germany is also maintained. In December of that year Pan Am became the first US carrier to link the USA and Saudi Arabia directly, with a same aircraft New York (JFK)-Frankfurt-Riyadh service. The current livery was proposed by Airbus Industrie to coincide with the delivery of the first A300s, and is now worn fleetwide. Regarded as one of the most effective liveries of today, the new image employs a plain white fuselage down to wing level, with huge 'Pan Am' titles in blue. The historic globe logo on the tail encompasses almost the entire fin. A fleet of Boeing 727, 737, 747, Airbus A300 and A310 aircraft is maintained. An order for the A320 has been cancelled with delivery positions being sold to Braniff. The ICAO call sign is 'CLIPPER'. *(B.T. Richards)*

PHILIPPINE AIRLINES (PR/PAL)

Philippines

Philippine Air Lines was founded in early 1941, and commenced limited internal operations on March 15 of that year. These were interrupted a few months later by the Second World War. It was not until February 14 1946, using war surplus Douglas DC-3s, did the carrier resume operations. International lines were initiated the following year. Long-range routes were suspended in 1951, and until 1961 PAL only operated within the Philippine Islands and to Hong Kong. Today the airline operates scheduled passenger and cargo services over a 41-point domestic system, together with international flights to Singapore, Kuala Lumpur, Taipei (CKS), Hong Kong, Honolulu, San Francisco, Los Angeles, Chicago, Tokyo (NRT), Melbourne, Sydney, Brisbane, Ho Chi Minh City, Bangkok, Karachi, Rome, Frankfurt, Amsterdam, Paris (ORY), Zurich, Beijing, Xiamen, Dhahran, Dubai and London (LGW). State shareholding in PAL was 24.6 per cent until November 1977, when the Government State Insurance System acquired the seventy-four per cent interest held by Rubicom (owned by the Toda family). Government holding is now 99.7 per cent. The airline operates a fleet of Shorts 360, BAe 1-11, A300, DC-10, NAMC YS-11, and Boeing 747 aircraft. PAL's latest livery, as currently being repainted on all the company's fleet, takes its colours from the crimson and blue national flag. A rising sun 'breaks out' from right to left on the tail, with the rest of the fuselage being painted pure white. Black 'Philippines' titling adorns the forward upper deck, whilst the national flag is situated behind the rear door. A Boeing 747-2F6B, is seen here at Paris (ORY), adorned in the latest livery. The aircraft was operating flight PR743 to Manila, via Amsterdam, Dubai and Bangkok. The carrier's ICAO call sign is 'PHILIPPINE'. *(K.G. Wright)*

QANTAS AIRWAYS (QF/QFA)

Australia

Qantas can trace its history back to November 16 1920, when the company was founded as Queensland & Northern Territory Aerial Services. The following year saw the start of charter operations and pleasure trips. The Avro 504K was Qantas' first aircraft. G-AUBG was used mainly for air taxi flights, joy rides and share sales tours, as well as being a reserve machine for the mail run until it was sold in November 1926. November 2 1922 saw the inaugural flight between Charleville and Cloncurry. It was flown in two stages to avoid the midday heat, with an overnight stop at Longreach. International services to Singapore were initiated in 1934, and by 1947 Qantas was flying to London. There then followed a rapid expansion period with destinations including Tokyo, Manila, Calcutta and Hong Kong coming on line. Commencing January 14 1958, Qantas inaugurated a round-the-world service. Using the Super G Constellation, flights departed Sydney for Honolulu, and from there touched down in San Francisco, New York, London, Cairo, Bahrain, Calcutta, Singapore, Perth and Melbourne, before arriving back in Sydney. The company received its first jet equipment in July 1959, in the form of a Boeing 707-138. It was the initial unit of an order for seven aircraft.

The Series 100 was, from 1967, replaced by the more powerful, Series 300. The early 1970s saw Qantas take possession of its first Boeing 747, the sole type to be utilized by the airline until the 1980s. Today, the company links Australia with Europe, the Middle and Far East, Africa, Asia and North America. A fleet of Boeing 747-200, -300 and SPs is utilized, as well as examples of the Boeing 767-200 and 300. An outstanding order for the Boeing 747-400 is eagerly awaited, as it will allow the company to offer one stop flights to Australia, with a full passenger load. In June 1985 a new livery was unveiled. A creation of the Lunn Design Group of Sydney, a dynamic and proudly Australian image is conjured up by a sleek white kangaroo which is contained within an all-red tail fin. This continues around the lower part of the tail fin and is trimmed in gold at the leading edge, adding elegance and sophistication. The rest of the fuselage is white, with the Qantas name in black lettering near the forward passenger door. The tail design is also on the engines, which are natural metal on the 747s, and white on the 767s. The company's ICAO call sign is 'QANTAS'. *(Qantas Airways)*

ROYAL AIR MAROC (AT/RAM)

Morocco

Royal Air Maroc was formed in June 1953 as Compagnie Cherifienne de Transports Aeriens. The carrier had been brought about through the merger of Societe Air Atlas and Air Maroc; the present title was adopted in 1957, to coincide with the country's independence. Stockholders in the company are the Moroccan Government (with 89.84 per cent), Air France, Compagnie Generale Transatlantique, and Aviaco. Today, the Moroccan flag carrier maintains scheduled services from the capital, Casablanca, and also Tangier, to domestic points, as well as to destinations in Europe, the Middle East, North and South America. Charter and inclusive tour flights are also undertaken. Royal Air Maroc's fleet consists of Boeing 707, 727, 737, 747 and 757 types. A single example of each of the Boeing 747-200 and 747SP-44 is utilized for high density and transatlantic services. The company's livery has a centrepiece which is displayed, in green, on the tail as a shooting star; taken from the national flag. The star's bright red tail encircles bold 'RAM' lettering. Lower case 'Royal Air Maroc' titles, again in red, adorn the upper forward fuselage; in English on the starboard and Arabic on the port. Below that is a decorative green and red windowline which has been allowed to taper at both ends. Undersides are left a natural metal on the Boeing 747s and 757s, whilst a grey paint is applied to the 727s and 737s. The company's 'SP' was purchased from South African Airways on March 14 1985, whilst the Boeing 747-200 was purpose-built for RAM, and was delivered on September 29 1978, as an SCD/Combi aircraft. CN-RMS, the 747SP-44, is depicted here on the tarmac at Casablanca Airport. The carrier's ICAO call sign is 'MAROCAIR'. *(Flying Colours)*

ROYAL JORDANIAN
AIRLINES (RJ/RJA)

Jordan

Royal Jordanian, formerly known until December 1986, as Alia, is the national flag carrier of the Middle Eastern state of Jordan. It was founded in December 1963 to succeed Jordan Airways, which itself had only been operating for two years. Originally called Alia, after King Hussein's daughter, a name which also means 'High Flying', the company inaugurated scheduled passenger operations between several Middle Eastern capitals and its base at Amman. Today services are maintained to various European cities, as well as those in Asia, the Far East, North Africa and North America. A fleet of Boeing 707, 727, 747, L-1011 Tristar, A310 and A320 aircraft is maintained. Royal Jordanian has several subsidiaries, these include Arab Wings, Royal Tours, Royal Jordanian Hospitality Services, Arab Air Cargo, Arab Air Services, the Royal Falcons, the Gateway Hotel, Royal Jordanian Boutique, Jordan Express Tourist Transport and Duty Free Shop. Several experimental colourschemes were evaluated before Royal approval was finally granted, in late 1986, to the livery that is now worn fleetwide. With a theme of Jordanian

Regality, the resulting scheme represents one of today's most stylish airline images. A dark grey covers the entire upper fuselage with the underside being painted white. Below the windowline is a thick gold cheatline that runs the entire length of the aircraft. A thin pink line is situated atop the windows, again travelling the length of the fuselage. Gold 'Royal Jordanian' titles, in upper case, adorn the front fuselage. Both the English and Arabic language is used, with the former being utilized first, followed by the latter on the port side, and the reverse is seen on the starboard. The Jordanian flag is situated towards the rear. On the centre of the tail fin is an impressive gold crown, whilst the top of the fin is painted bright red. Black streaks cover the vertical stabilizer. JY-AFA, the company's sole Boeing 747-200 SCD, is seen here at Amsterdam's Schipol Airport. The aircraft had recently arrived from Amman on its nonstop flight RJ261, and is depicted here taxiing to its arrival gate, C16. The carrier's ICAO call sign is 'JORDANIAN'. *(K.G. Wright)*

SABENA — BELGIAN WORLD AIRLINES (SN/SAB)

Belgium

Sabena, the Belgian national airline, was formed over sixty-five years ago on May 23 1923 to succeed SNETA. The company had previously operated route proving services within Africa for three years. A European network was set up, followed by routes to and within the Belgian Congo (Zaire). Sabena has a number of subsidiaries, these include: Sobelair, Societe Transair International, Sodehotel, Compagnie des Grandes Hotels Africairns, Compagnie Internationale de Gestion-Bruxelles, Compagnie Rwandaise d'Hotellerie et de Tourisme, Sabena Catering Services, Airtour 2000, Belgian Fuelling and Services, Sabena Interservice Centre, and Delta Air Transport. Today Sabena operates an extensive network of scheduled passenger and cargo services to points in Europe and the Middle and Far East, and also to Johannesburg, Montreal, New York (JFK), Atlanta, Detroit, Chicago, Boston and Toronto. The company has recently introduced services to Niamey (Niger), Lome (Togo), Cotonou (Benin), and Luanda (Angola), underlying its African heritage. A fleet of Airbus A310, Boeing-737-200 and -300, Boeing 747-100 and -300, Douglas DC-10-30, SIAI Marchetti SF/260, and Embraer 121 Xingu aircraft is operated. Orders for the Boeing 737-400 and 737-500 are currently outstanding. These will replace the Series 200 aircraft already in service with the Belgian flag carrier, and its subsidiary, Sobelair. With the delivery of the first A310 to Sabena in March 1984, a subtle modernisation of the familiar colourscheme was unveiled, which has since been adopted fleetwide. A lighter blue cheatline extends along the fuselage length, trimmed either side by narrow pinstripes in the same colour. Matching Sabena titles are displayed on the upper fuselage in a new style, but are still followed by the flag and 'Belgian World Airlines' sub titles. The tail fin remains unaltered, with the 'S' dissecting a large white disc. The lower fuselage is painted grey on all members of the fleet. One of Sabena's two 747-100s can be seen here on approach to London's Gatwick Airport. At the time it was operating a joint flight agreement with the former British Caledonian Airways, on services to Atlanta. The company's ICAO call sign is 'SABENA'. *(K.G. Wright)*

SAUDIA — SAUDI ARABIAN AIRLINES (SV/SDI)

Saudi Arabia

Saudia, the national flag carrier of the Kingdom of Saudi Arabia, was formed in 1945 by the Saudia Arabian Government, and began operations in 1947; using a fleet of Douglas DC-3s. The airline today, operates scheduled passenger and cargo services to twenty-three domestic and forty-four international destinations. Overseas destinations are served from Jeddah, Riyadh, and Dhahran. Points are flown to in Europe, Africa, the Middle and Far East, as well as to the USA. Passenger and cargo charters are also undertaken. Saudia's livery, unchanged for some years, still appears both modern and stylish. It features a double sub-divided cheatline arrangement in two shades of green, above two shades of blue. These are separated by a narrow white stripe. The white upper fuselage contrasts greatly with the polished natural metal undersides, and displays a complicated title arrangement. This appears in both English and Arabic, with 'Saudia' in one script and the secondary 'Saudi Arabian Airlines' titles in the other, reversed on the opposite side. An all-green fin carries the traditional Saudia logo, which basically consists of two crossed swords before a palm tree on a white inverted triangle. Below is small 'Saudia' lettering in English on the starboard side and Arabic on the port. The airline operates a fleet of Boeing 737s, 747s, L-1011 Tristars and A300s. Various executive aircraft are used for VIP flights. A Boeing 747-168B is seen here on approach to London Heathrow Airport's runway 27 right. It was operating Saudia's nonstop flight SV049 from Jeddah. It should be noted that 747-300s have since replaced the smaller Series 100 aircraft. The carrier's ICAO call sign is 'SAUDIA'. *(K.G. Wright)*

SCANDINAVIAN AIRLINES SYSTEM (SK/SAS)

Denmark, Norway, Sweden

The owners of SAS are, in proportion of 2:2:3, Det Danske Luftfartselskap (Danish Airlines), Det Norske Luftfartselskap (Norwegian Airlines), and Aerotransport (Swedish Airlines). These three limited companies are in turn, through shareholdings, owned fifty per cent by private individuals or enterprises, and fifty per cent by their respective national governments. SAS was formed in 1946 to operate scheduled transatlantic services. All of the routes flown by the three airlines are now operated by this single company. Wholly-owned subsidiaries are SAS Service Partner (catering and offshore services), SAS International Hotels, SAS Informational Reservation System, and SAS Leisure. Scanair is an associate company, owned jointly by ABA, DDL, and DNL, which operates charter and inclusive tour services. Other airlines which SAS has an interest in are Danair (fifty-seven per cent), Linjeflyg (fifty per cent), Greenlandair (twenty-five per cent), Helikopter Service (five per cent), and Wideroe (twenty-two per cent). A fleet of DC-9, DC-10, Boeing 767, F-27 and MD81, MD82 and MD83 aircraft is maintained. Delivery of the MD11 is awaited. The current SAS livery was given board approval in 1983, in preference to two similar designs, and is now worn fleetwide. A white overall fuselage has, as its highlight, a rhombus in the national colours of the three participating nations, Denmark, Norway and Sweden (reading from the front). Basic 'Scandinavian' titles are in dark blue, outlined in gold, as is the 'SAS' tail logo, and the three national flags appear on the rear engines, or rear fuselage (reading Denmark, Norway, Sweden, from left to right). The Scandinavian carrier no longer operates Boeing 747s. Following a rationalisation of the SAS fleet, they have been replaced by DC-10s and Boeing 767s. This example, a Series 283B, is seen here at Stockholm's Arlanda Airport. The carrier's ICAO call sign is 'SCANDINAVIAN'. *(K.G. Wright)*

SINGAPORE AIRLINES (SQ/SIA)

Singapore

Singapore Airlines was formed on January 28 1972, as the wholly Government-owned national airline of Singapore, to succeed the jointly operated Malaysia-Singapore Airlines. Operations began on October 1 of that year. In November 1985 some sixteen per cent of SIA's expanded stock was sold to local and international investors. This reduced the Government's holding to seventy-three per cent, with a further subsequent reduction to fifty-five per cent in June 1987. The carrier's first two Boeing 747-400 aircraft were delivered in December 1988, and began nonstop Singapore to London (LHR) services in early 1989. SIA's first 747 pure freighter entered service in August of that year; operating to Europe, the Far East, and the south west Pacific. Subsidiary companies include Tradewinds, Singapore Airport Terminal Services, Singapore Engine Overhaul Centre, Singapore Aviation and General Insurance, Singapore International Software Services, Aeroformation Asia, and Singapore Properties. Scheduled passenger and cargo services are operated from Singapore to Auckland, Adelaide, Christchurch, Darwin, Port

Moresby, Brisbane, Sydney, Melbourne, Perth, Honolulu, Los Angeles, San Francisco, Tokyo (NRT), Osaka, Seoul, Taipei (CKS), Hong Kong, Manila, Bandar Seri Begawan, Jakarta, Fukuoka, Medan, Kuala Lumpur, Kuantan, Penang, Bangkok, Colombo, Cairo, Calcutta, Kathmandu, Denpasar, Delhi, Dhaka, Male, Manchester, Beijing, Shanghai, Karachi, Madras, Bombay, Mauritius, Dubai, Dhahran, Bahrain, Athens, Rome, Vienna, Istanbul, Zurich, Frankfurt, Paris (CDG), Amsterdam, Copenhagen, Brussels and London (LHR). A fleet of Boeing 747, 757 and Airbus A310 aircraft is maintained. A white fuselage displays shortened cheatlines in midnight blue and yellow; below blue upper case 'Singapore Airlines' titles. A large stylised yellow bird looks down from the mainly blue fin, which is repeated in miniature on each engine. Note, that the 747-300s display large 'Big Top' lettering on the forward fuselage, whilst the A310s have the legend '3Ten' adjacent to the cockpit windows. 9V-SKA, a 747-300, is seen here at Singapore's Changi Airport. The carrier's ICAO call sign is 'SINGAPORE'. *(K.G. Wright)*

SWISSAIR (SR/SWR)   Switzerland

Swissair was formed on March 26 1931, when Ad Astra Aero and Basle Air Transport were amalgamated. The former company was founded in 1919, and began flying boat operations in Switzerland, before pioneering international routes. Today Swissair operates an extensive network of scheduled passenger and cargo services, linking 107 cities in seventy-two countries in Europe, North and South America, Africa, and the Middle and Far East. The airline has a number of aviation-related subsidiaries, including Balair, CTA, and Swissair Associated Companies. It also owns catering, hotel, tourism, real estate and insurance firms as well. Swissair is a partner with SAS, KLM and UTA in the KSSU consortium; which was formed to co-operate in technical and equipment pooling. During the Spring of 1988, the Swiss national flag carrier became the first airline to put the Fokker 100 into commercial service. It was also the initial company to operate the Airbus A310-322 Intercontinental, in February 1986. Approximately seventy-eight per cent of share capital is held by private interests and the rest by public institutions. A fleet of DC-9, DC-10, MD81, Fokker 100, A310 and Boeing 747 aircraft is maintained. An order for the MD11 is awaited, with deliveries commencing in May 1990. It should be noted that some scheduled passenger flights are operated on behalf of Swissair, by Crossair, using Saab 340A equipment. The Swiss flag covers the tail, boldly stating the carrier's country of origin. This is complemented by bright red 'Swissair' titles over a white fuselage top. Straight twin cheatlines in brown (upper) and black (lower) extend from nose to tail below the window level. The lower fuselage is finished in grey on the A310s, whilst natural metal is the order on the other types; some of which are highly polished. A Boeing 747-357B is seen here whilst on approach to Zurich. The carrier's ICAO call sign is 'SWISSAIR'. *(Swissair)*

SOUTH AFRICAN AIRWAYS (SA/SAA)

South Africa

The carrier was formed in February 1934, when the Union Government took over assets and liabilities of Union Airways, and to operate as a division of South African Railways, using Junkers F13s. The following year the carrier acquired South West African Airways. Today the airline is owned and controlled by the Government of South Africa and falls under the jurisdiction of South African Transport Services. SAA currently operates scheduled passenger and cargo services to domestic points, together with regional services to Harare, Gaborone Moroni, Bulawayo, Windhoek, Maputo, Mauritius, Reunion, Victoria Falls, Lusaka, and Lilongwe. International lines link Johannesburg, Durban and Cape Town, with Rio de Janeiro, Hong Kong, Ilha do Sal, Lisbon, Taipei (CKS), Madrid, Rome, Athens, Abidjan, Vienna, Zurich, Frankfurt, Paris (ORY), Brussels, Amsterdam, London (LHR) and Tel Aviv. A fleet of Boeing 737, 747 and Airbus A300 aircraft is maintained. An order for the A320 is outstanding; these aircraft eventually replacing the older Boeing 737 types. The South African Airways livery can certainly be classed as bilingual, since all the titling on the port side is in English, and on the starboard, in Afrikaans. This even goes down to the company logo which reads 'SAA' on one side, and 'SAL' on the other. The distinctive orange tail fin displays a leaping springbok in blue, outlined in white, and a dark blue 'straight through' windowline that runs parallel with a narrower line in bright orange below. A highly polished underside adds a stylish touch, although on the Airbus fleet, these are painted in grey. ZS-SPF, a Boeing 747SP-44, is seen here on arrival at Zurich. The aircraft had just completed a flight from Johannesburg as SA246, routing via Madrid. The carrier's ICAO call sign is 'SPRINGBOK.' *(K.G. Wright)*

SYRIANAIR (RB/SYR)

Syria

Syrian Arab Airlines was founded in October 1961 by the Syrian Government, to succeed Syrian Airways (formed in 1946). Its aim was to be the country's national flag carrier and to operate both domestic and regional scheduled services. Today the airline operates an extensive network of scheduled passenger and cargo flights from Damascus to Aleppo, Latakia, Kameshli and Deirezzar within Syria, and from Damascus to Delhi, Karachi, Bombay, Sharjah, Bahrain, Abu Dhabi, Doha, Dhahran, Riyadh, Kuwait, Jeddah, Sana'a, Tehran, Larnaca, Athens, Beirut, Instanbul, Tripoli, Tunis, Algiers, Casablanca, Bucharest, Sofia, Rome, Erevan, Budapest, Prague, Moscow, Copenhagen, Berlin, Frankfurt, Munich and Paris (ORY). A diverse fleet of Boeing 727, 747SP, Tupolev 134, TU-154, SE-210 Caravelle, Ilyushin 76, Antonov 26, Yakovlev Yak-40 and Falcon 20F aircraft is maintained. Unusually, the national carrier does not take its colours from the country's red, white and black flag, but instead uses a bright Mediterranean blue cheatline over a predominantly white fuselage to complement the mixture of American and Soviet airliner equipment. The titling arrangement on the starboard side has blue 'Syrianair' lettering in Arabic followed by English, reversed on the port side, and the tail fin displays a stylised mystical bird gliding across a blue sun. It should be noted that some types sport Syrian Air titles in two words in black lettering. Pictured prior to the cessation of diplomatic relations between the United Kingdom and Syria, and the withdrawal of the London (LHR)-Damascus route, Boeing 747SP-94, YK-AHB, 'Arab Solidarity', can be seen here departing London's Heathrow Airport on flight RB402. The carrier's ICAO call sign is 'SYRIANAIR'. *(B.T. Richards)*

THAI AIRWAYS
INTERNATIONAL (TG/THA)

Thailand

Thai International was formed in August 1959 as a subsidiary of the domestic carrier, Thai Airways, with technical, managerial, and equipment assistance being provided by the Scandinavian carrier, SAS. In 1960 flights were inaugurated to nine overseas destinations within the South East Asia region. Intercontinental services were added in 1971, to Australia, followed by flights to Europe the following year. On April 1 1977, the Thai Government bought out SAS's fifteen per cent holding, and now owns ninety-four per cent of the airline. An extensive network of scheduled passenger and cargo services is maintained, and these link Bangkok with forty-three destinations in thirty-one countries throughout South East Asia, the Middle East, Australia, Europe and the USA. April 1 1988 saw the merger of Thai Airways, the domestic carrier, and Thai International. The former company had itself been formed on November 1 1951, by the merger of Siamese Airways and Pacific Overseas Airlines (Siam). It operated an extensive domestic network that radiated from Bangkok to over twenty destinations. Additional services were

flown to Vientiane, Penang and Kuala Lumpur. Today Thai International's combined fleet consists of Shorts 330, Shorts 360, BAe 748, Boeing 737, 747, DC-10, Airbus A300 and A310 equipment. Airbus A330 and MD11 aircraft will be delivered during the 1990s, thus replacing the older DC-10s in the fleet. The majestic Thai International livery was created over thirteen years ago, in 1975, by Walter Landor Associates, under a brief that called for a reflection of Thai heritage in both colour and form. A huge Royal Orchid motif covers the tail fin, in shades of magenta, gold and purple, and is repeated on the forward fuselage at the head of a broad cheatline which is similarly coloured. Abbreviated 'Thai' lettering appears near the forward passenger door in purple and the national flag is displayed at the top of the fin. It should be noted that the registration is colour co-ordinated and is applied in purple towards the rear of the fuselage. The carrier's ICAO call sign is 'THAI INTER'.

(Thai Airways International)

TOWER AIR
(FF/TOW)

United States of America

Tower Air was formed in August 1982 to operate the passenger services previously undertaken by Metro International Airways. The carrier began scheduled operations on former MIA routes, linking New York (JFK) with Brussels and Tel Aviv in March 1983. Today Tower Air operates scheduled passenger services from New York (JFK) to Tel Aviv, Brussels, Oslo and Stockholm. Charters to destinations that include Zurich, Paris (ORY), Rome, and Athens are also undertaken. Special contract charters are also flown on behalf of the United States Military Airlift Command (MAC). A total of four Boeing 747-100s are operated, one of which was purchased from Metro, upon the company's foundation, in November 1983. Another two were delivered in 1985; these aircraft being purchased from Avianca and Transamerica. Whilst the fourth was delivered during 1988, having been purchased from TWA. Boeing 747-127, 'Sam', N601BN, still retains Metro International's livery. Consisting of a deep blue cheatline and tail, the aircraft is also adorned with matching blue 'Tower Air' titling and fin logo. N602FF and N603FF, 'Suzie', display the 'official' company livery. Although simple and becoming more commonplace, vast dark blue 'Tower Air' titles stretch across the forward fuselage, having been facilitated by the adoption of a pure white fuselage. The lettering is repeated sloping up the fin below a US flag. N93117 retains its former TWA red, below window level cheatline, whilst 'Tower Air' titles appear sloping up the fin, below the US flag, on the forward fuselage. One of the airline's aircraft is seen here at Brussels Zaventum Airport. The carrier's ICAO call sign is 'TEE AIR'. *(K.G. Wright)*

TRANS WORLD AIRLINES (TW/TWA)

United States of America

Trans World Airlines was founded on October 1 1930, as Trans-continental and Western Air, through a merger of a part of Western Air Express, TAT-Maddux, and Pittsburgh Aviation Industries Corporation. The present name was adopted in May 1950. In January 1979, Trans World Corporation became the parent company of TWA. In December 1982 TWC shareholders voted to sell TWA, and on February 1 1984, the carrier was established as a separate, entirely publicly owned, company. On September 26, 1985, TWA was taken over by New York investor Carl Icahn, who acquired fifty-two per cent of the company's shares. The airline merged with St. Louis-based Ozark Air Lines in 1987. Today, Trans World Airlines operates an extensive network of scheduled passenger services in the USA, where the carrier serves over 100 destinations. Transatlantic services are operated to a large number of points in Europe and the Middle East. The airline's main hubs are at New York (JFK) and St. Louis. A fleet of Boeing 727, 747, 767, Tristar, DC-9 and MD82 aircraft is maintained. In 1988, the carrier

and Gulf Air signed an agreement whereby TWA's aircraft would be used in conjunction with Gulf Air on flights to the Middle East. Services from the USA to the Middle East are staged via London (LHR). The airline's colourscheme was officially unveiled on November 30 1974. This replaced the traditional 'twin globe' scheme, which had remained unchanged for over ten years, apart from the Trans World titling which now appears in solid red; replacing the previous red outline. Thin red cheatlines commence at the nose, under the black anti-dazzle panels, and proceed along the white fuselage below the windows. They then widen as they go, and ultimately wrap around under the fuselage. The fin displays the white 'TWA' logo, reversed out of the red centre section, which varies in shape from type to type. It should be noted that the US flag is situated at the top of the fin on most types, but on those with a T-tail is featured alongside the registration. A Boeing 747-131 is seen here at Zurich. The carrier's ICAO call sign is 'TWA', however, there are occasions when 'TRANS WORLD' is used. *(K.G. Wright)*

UNITED AIRLINES (UA/UAL)

United States of America

United Airlines was formed on March 27 1931, as a management company of four pioneer airlines; these being Boeing Air Transport, Pacific Air Transport, National Air Transport, and Varney Airlines (founded in 1926). Capital Airlines was absorbed in 1961. Today, United, ranked as one of the world's largest carriers, completed the purchase of Pan Am's Pacific Division on February 10 1986. Under the terms of the agreement, United took over eighteen aircraft, spare parts, property, facilities and over 2,600 Pan Am employees associated with the Pacific Division. In June 1986 the airline established formal feeder agreements with four US regional carriers. These being Air Wisconsin, Aspen Airways, Presidential Airlines and West Air, all of which fly under the 'United Express' banner. The airline operates an extensive system of scheduled passenger and cargo routes, linking more than 160 cities in the United States, Canada, and Mexico. International services are operated to the Far East, Australia, New Zealand and the Caribbean. The carrier has three primary system traffic and route hubs: Chicago's O'Hare Airport, Denver's Stapleton Airport and San Francisco International Airport. A fleet of Boeing 727, 737, 747, 757,

767, DC-8 and DC-10 aircraft is maintained. An outstanding order for a quantity of the Boeing 747-400 is eagerly awaited. The airline is a main subsidiary of UAL Inc, which owns Westin Hotels, GAB Business Services and Hawaii's Mauna Kea Properties. United has an outstanding livery. Patriotic red and blue is used for the large 'U' tail motif and for the main cheatlines, brightened by a third line in orange. The 'U' logo is repeated after the recently enlarged black 'United' fuselage lettering. Most aircraft in the fleet sport a white upper and lower fuselage finish, although some have a natural metal lower half. Seen here at New York's JFK International Airport is Boeing 747SP-21, N539PA. This particular aircraft is unusual in that it is wearing a hybrid livery. Having just been purchased from Pan Am, it still sports that airline's cheatline, and a national flag on the tail. However, United Airlines titles and tail logo have been added. This aircraft is being prepared for a departure to Hong Kong as UA17, via Seattle and Seoul. It should be noted this 'SP' has since been re-registered N148UA. The carrier's ICAO call sign is 'UNITED'. *(K.G. Wright)*

UNITED PARCEL SERVICE (UPS)

United States of America

United Parcel Service was founded in 1907 as a messenger service. It was briefly in the air express business from 1929 to 1931 on the US West Coast. In 1953 a two-day 'UPS-AIR' service (now UPS 2nd Day Air) was established between major US cities. In 1982 UPS entered the overnight small package market and now serves more US points than any other carrier. Flights to Europe were introduced in October 1985. Today the airline provides a scheduled network of parcel services throughout the USA, Europe and Japan. The services offered are 'UPS Next Day Air' (delivery to every address in the forty-eight contiguous states, Hawaii and Puerto Rico), and 'UPS 2nd Day Air' (same territory, plus Anchorage, Alaska). 'UPS International Air' links the forty-eight states with Europe and Japan. Customer brokerage services are offered on international shipments. The company's aircraft are also available for charter and cargo services. The carrier's air hub is at Louisville, Kentucky. A fleet of Douglas DC-8, Boeing 727, 747F, 757PF, and Swearingen Expediter aircraft is maintained. Today, the company serves shippers and consignees throughout the United States, Canada, Europe, Australasia and East Asia. United Parcel Service's colour-scheme must be unique, in as much as it used chocolate brown as a predominant colour. The airline livery comprises a conventional broad windowline which eventually covers the whole tail fin. The logo, a shield displaying 'UPS' lettering beneath a wrapped parcel, appears on the tail in gold outline, and bold brown 'United Parcel Service' lettering is carried on the forward upper fuselage. N9675, a Boeing 747-123F SCD, is seen here at Ontario on October 21 1984. It should be noted that this aircraft has since been re-registered N675UP. *(Author's Collection)*

UTA (UT/UTA)

France

UTA was founded on October 1 1963 following the merger of UAT and TAI. Today the carrier is France's largest independent carrier. The airline operates scheduled passenger and cargo services from Paris (CDG), Nice, Marseille, Lyon, and Toulouse, to twenty-three points in Africa, to Bahrain and Muscat in the Middle East, to Los Angeles, San Francisco, and Honolulu in the USA, and to Tokyo (NRT) and eight other points in the Asia-Pacific region. Charter and inclusive tour services are also provided. UTA has the distinction of being the world's only round-the-world passenger carrying airline. Flights commence in Paris, and from there the aircraft travels to Muscat, Colombo, Kuala Lumpur, Singapore, Jakarta, Sydney, Noumea, Papeete, and San Francisco, before arriving back in the French capital. In association with London City Airways, flights are maintained to the London STOL-port (LCY), using DHC-7 aircraft. UTA is a subsidiary of Chargeous Reunis, which has a 62.5 per cent holding. Companies in which the airline has a stake, include

SODETRAF, Air Inter, CRMA, Revima, UTH (hotels), Compagnie Aeromaritime d'Affretement, UTA Services Tahiti (airport services), and holiday villages in Polynesia and New Caledonia. A fleet of Boeing 747 and DC-10 aircraft is maintained. Delivery of Boeing 747-400 and A340 types is awaited. UTA was one of the first carriers to adopt a modern white overall fuselage colouring; in this case it features passenger doors highlighted in bright green. The whole fin and rearmost part of the fuselage is in dark blue, with a small 'UTA' logo appearing inconspicuously at the top of the tail. Huge titles in the same colour adorn the fuselage; so large are these that they are visible from the ground on overflying aircraft. Pure-freight aircraft have an all-white fuselage without green highlights, but wear additional blue cargo titles. Some of the Boeing 747-300s have a 'Big Boss' legend on the upper forward fuselage. F-GDUA can be seen here during a test flight prior to delivery. The carrier's ICAO call sign is 'UTA'. *(UTA)*

VARIG (RG/VRG)

Brazil

Varig can trace its history back over fifty years to its foundation in May 1927. Its aim was to operate a single Dornier WAL flying boat over the domestic Porto Alegre-Rio Grande route, succeeding the former Kondor Syndikat. The airline subsequently absorbed several other airlines, including the domestic operator Aero Geral (1951), the Real consortium (1961), and Panair do Brazil's equipment and international routes in 1965. Cruzeiro was acquired in 1975. Today, Varig operates an extensive network of routes throughout South and Central America, and to the USA, Europe, Africa, and Japan. Domestic operators Cruzeiro and Rio-Sul are subsidiaries. Most of the company's shares are held by the foundation of employees and executives. A fleet of Boeing 707, 727, 737, 747, 767, A300, DC-10 and L-188 Electra aircraft is maintained. Delivery of the MD11 is awaited. The predominant dark blue colourscheme is obtained from the national flag and colours the broad cheatline, which curves round the aircraft's chin and also features a 'seam effect', created by white pinstripes at window level. The famous compass logo is displayed on the fin, above black 'Varig' titling. However, on the fuselage, the company name is repeated in blue alongside the Brazilian flag, and 'Brasil' lettering in black. The overall livery is adapted slightly to fit the shapes of the other aircraft in the fleet. The only really notable exception being the application of the 'flying figurehead' logo positioned above the cheatline on the 747s and most DC-10s in natural metal, the A300s in grey, and some of the DC-10s in a more visually pleasing white. A Boeing 747-2L5B SCD, is seen here at Frankfurt Main in October 1986. The carrier's ICAO call sign is 'VARIG'. It should be noted that whilst operating flights for Rotatur, the designation DR/RTR is used, along with the ICAO call sign 'ROTATUR'. *(B.T. Richards)*

VIRGIN ATLANTIC
AIRWAYS (VS/VIR)

United Kingdom

When Richard Branson started Virgin Atlantic on June 22 1984, little did he realize that within three years he would be operating two Boeing 747s on transatlantic flights, two daily European services, and have carried well over one million transatlantic passengers. From those early days, Virgin Atlantic Airways has grown from strength to strength. Starting with a single 747-200, (G-VIRG, or more affectionately known as 'The Maiden Voyager'), and a daily service to New York (EWR), the airline then quickly added Maastricht in Holland to its route structure. This was supported with a daily BAe 1-11 service, although this type was replaced with a Viscount. This route was originally regarded as a feeder for the transatlantic run, but it has now established itself as a successful service in its own right. In April 1986, the Gatwick-Miami route began operating. Another 747-200, G-VGIN (named 'The Scarlet Lady'), had to be purchased. This opened up a second gateway for Virgin into the USA. In June 1987, Virgin introduced a new service to Dublin from Luton. The route was so popular, that by the fourth month of flights, the company had carried its 50,000th passenger across the Irish Sea. It was decided at that time to replace the

Viscount with two Boeing 727 aircraft, leased from Club Air, of Ireland. Unfortunately, this carrier ceased operations, and Viscounts were again used. Occasional leases were undertaken from Paramount, utilizing MD80 aircraft. Commencing May 26 1988, the company inaugurated its first charter flights, to Orlando. Using one of its 747s, Virgin operated a once-weekly service to the Floridian destination. June 17 saw the company open a Luton-Maastricht line, in addition to the Gatwick service. A daily round trip is offered using Viscount aircraft. New routes have been awarded to New York (JFK) and Los Angeles. These having been designated to Virgin following the British Airways-British Caledonian merger. Approval for a new service to Tokyo (NRT) was granted in August 1988, for scheduled flights beginning on May 1 1989. G-TKYO, Boeing 747-212B, 'Maiden Japan', was added for the Far East route. The Virgin colourscheme is one of the most striking in the world, and is the only airline ever to paint its aircraft using the full company livery. An orange 'straight-through' windowline extends below the similarly-coloured 'Virgin' signature near the cockpit windows, and is repeated in white on the all-orange fin. A 'Scarlet Lady' appears on its 747s. The airline operates a fleet of Boeing 747 aircraft. Its ICAO call sign is 'VIRGIN.' *(Virgin Atlantic)*